NGA IWI (

1 0 0 0   Y e a r s   o f

MICHAEL KING

REED

Established in 1907, Reed Publishing (NZ) Ltd
is New Zealand's largest book publisher, with over 300 titles in print.

For details on all these books visit our website:
www.reed.co.nz

Published by Reed Books, a division of Reed Publishing (NZ) Ltd,
39 Rawene Rd, Birkenhead, Auckland.
Associated companies, branches and representatives throughout the world.

ISBN 0 7900 0800 9

© 1997 Michael King

The author asserts his moral rights in the work.
First published 1997
Revised edition 2001

Printed in New Zealand

Contents

For
Heeni Wharemaru and Marjorie Rau-Kupa:
Beloved Friends and Keepers of the Flame

Introduction

In the mid-1980s, after more than a decade in the field, I announced that I was vacating the arena of Maori history. This was in the wake of a television documentary series, a doctoral thesis, three biographies, books on tattooing and reporting Maori activities, a general history, contributions to other volumes and the editing of two books by Maori authors.

I did not take this decision lightly. Nor was it a result of dissatisfaction on the part of iwi or individuals with whom I had worked in partnership. On the contrary, Maori colleagues remained friends and professional associates. But I viewed the Maori renaissance at that time as implying a wish to take control of analyses and expressions of Maori culture. I also hoped that by stepping aside I would encourage the emergence of more Maori authors.

Another decade on and that latter hope has scarcely been realised. In spite of promising books by Ranginui Walker, Buddy Mikaere and Lindsay Cox, most Maori history is still being written by Pakeha – albeit by scrupulous and well-equipped Pakeha such as Judith Binney, Anne Salmond and Angela Ballara. I have no complaint about this. The standard of their work is excellent. But I do regret that the resource claim industry, particularly the activities of the Waitangi Tribunal, has swallowed the talents of so many potential Maori authors. I take some comfort from the fact that Tribunal work has generated sufficient research for dozens of books on iwi and hapu history; and I trust that in due course they will be written and published.

For myself, I have for the most part kept the promise I made in 1985 – although I did write a book on Moriori of the Chatham Islands at their express request; and I participated in the Moriori claim to the Waitangi Tribunal. I have agreed to the publication of this present book because there is still no single-volume overview of Maori history and Maori-Pakeha relations based on professional research and readily available to general readers and students. It is a revised version of the text I wrote for the rather more elaborate *Māori, A Photographic and Social History*, first published in 1983. It represents not so much a re-entry into the field as a continuing interest in what was my first specialist subject. It has been updated to take into account the work of the authors I have mentioned, and that of Professor James Belich.

Michael King

CHAPTER ONE

TANGATA WHENUA

People of the Land

Maori have long been amused or offended by the notion that Maori history began with the arrival of Pakeha in New Zealand – as if there was no such thing as history until literate Europeans observed and recorded it. This notion has been strengthened by scholars' use of the expression 'prehistory' to describe the years prior to Maori-Pakeha contact.

It is, of course, nonsense. History does not come into existence with the birth of literature, although literature may well be part of the historical process. History is the story of the human occupation of a place compiled from surviving evidence. The three key features are occupation, evidence and story. New Zealand has had occupation, evidence of it and stories about it for at least 1,000 years. The evidence survives in the artifacts and structures of New Zealand Polynesian technology, and the stories in the oral traditions of surviving tribes, many of them committed to paper in the nineteenth and twentieth centuries, many of them still orally transmitted. The resulting combination might not be exhaustive and definitive, but what history is?

The apparently dismissive attitude to the earliest years of New Zealand settlement is reflected in the inadequate attention scholars have given it. Part of the explanation for this neglect lies in Western concepts of history, especially the insistence on working with contemporary documents; part in an unwillingness or an inability to tap Maori oral sources and documents written in Maori; part in the absence of professional Maori historians; and part in the relatively recent introduction of archaeology and anthropology to New Zealand and the small number of researchers in these disciplines. Consequently, the most pressing need in New Zealand historiography is a work which addresses itself to the earlier period; which locates, collates and analyses all the traditional, linguistic and archaeological evidence relating to the country's initial occupation, and the tribal movements and settlement patterns which followed that occupation and preceded European redis-covery. So-called prehistorians began working towards such a synthesis in the 1950s and 1960s. But since then the relatively few people working in archaeology have tended to turn their attention to more localised considerations. As an overview, this book can merely note the imbalance, not rectify it.

In this context, it is perhaps misleading to speak of 'Maori history'. Paradoxically there were no Maori in New Zealand before there were Europeans; or, at least, there was no race of people called 'Maori'. New Zealand Polynesians do not appear to have begun to use this expression until the 1840s; and they did not do so on a wide scale until early in the twentieth century. 'Maori' meant 'normal' or 'usual' − as in 'tangata Maori', an ordinary man. There was no need to distinguish such ordinary people from others until the land was shared by others; a group long separated from other races and cultures had no concepts of race or culture, nor, initially, the vocabulary to express them.

Pre-European New Zealanders identified themselves by hapu (sub-tribe) and by iwi or tribe. They had personal names. But the name of the founder of the hapu or iwi to which they belonged by descent, preceded by the prefix 'Ngati' (meaning 'descendants of') determined their identity, as did the place where they lived. The first question they would be asked by strangers was not *who* they were but where they were from. This was an inquiry about both place of habitation and identity. A person who lived on the banks of the Waikato River in the central North Island would announce this fact. He might then recite his genealogy back to Tamaoho, progenitor of his hapu; and then − if he was of senior lineage and well equipped in tribal knowledge − back to Hoturoa, captain of the *Tainui* canoe. He might then emphasise his wider affiliation to the Waikato confederation of tribes and their association with the river by reciting a whakatauki or tribal saying such as 'Waikato taniwharau, he piko he taniwha' – Waikato, river of a hundred bends, and on every one of them a taniwha. Metaphorically this also referred to Waikato the tribe, and the taniwha to the number of powerful chiefs belonging to the tribe and the number of fortifications along the river. Thus the whakatauki was an assertion of group pride as well as of personal identity.

The pre-tribal origins of the New Zealand Polynesians cannot be established with any precision from traditional sources alone. They had a series of myths and legends to account for the existence of New Zealand, which most referred to by using the names given for the North, South and Stewart Islands (Te Ika-a-Maui, Te Wai Pounamu, Rakiura). They also had a repository of mythology to account for their existence as men and women, and for the origin of the natural elements.

The Maori creation myths were shared in broad outline with Polynesians in other parts of the Pacific. Rangi the Sky Father had been joined in amorous embrace to Papa, the Earth Mother. In this clasp the world was in perpetual darkness, and the nakedness of Papa was covered with vegetation that thrived in dank moisture. The sons of Rangi and Papa constantly lamented the miserable conditions in which they were forced to live between their parents. Eventually they resolved to do something about them. One, Tu-matauenga, god of war, suggested that the parents would have to be killed to be separated. Tane-mahuta, god of the forest and later father of mankind, objected. No, he said. It would be sufficient to prise them apart and let the Sky stand above us and the Earth lie below. Let the Sky become a stranger but the Earth remain our nurturing Mother.

All but one of the sons agreed to this course and they took turns trying to bring about the separation. None succeeded until Tane-mahuta placed his shoulders against the Earth and his feet upon the Sky. Slowly and powerfully he straightened his body and his parents began to give way. The sinews with which they held each other tore and they cried out in pain. But Tane persisted. And in the end he succeeded in fixing the Sky above and the Earth below. As soon as this was done the children of Rangi and Papa knew light for the first time; and the children of Tane – the trees, birds and insects of the forest – were able to breathe, to see and to move.

The one son who had objected to the separation, Tawhiri-matea, was angered by the pain his parents had suffered and the regard with which Tane-mahuta was now held by other living things. So he followed Rangi to the realm above and there he begot his own offspring: wind, rain and storms. He unleashed these on the children of Tane in retribution. Then he hurled himself down from the skies as a hurricane and uprooted Tane's trees. Eventually, after attacking all his other brothers, Tawhiri-matea returned to the Sky whence he and his children would continue to descend from time to time to plague the Earth and her occupants.

It was Tane-mahuta who then created the first woman out of earth, Hine-ahu-one, and procreated with her. Their descendants, who also procreated, produced a line of men-like gods and god-like men. One of these, Maui, was credited with fishing up the North Island of New Zealand – an especially appropriate myth in the light of the island's relatively recent volcanic history. Maui was an archetypal hero throughout Polynesia. He was the last-born in his family so that in theory his rank was low. But he compensated for this by being far more resourceful and cunning than his brothers.

In the fish story (and there are many others) Maui smuggled himself aboard his brothers' canoe in Hawaiki, the traditional Polynesian homeland. They were annoyed by his trickery and wanted to return to shore. But by this time land was too far away so they continued with their planned fishing expedition. After the brothers had filled the canoe with their catch Maui produced his own hook, the barb of which was made from a fragment of his grandmother's jaw-bone. The brothers refused him bait so Maui struck his own nose and smeared the hook with his blood. He lowered his line and almost immediately hooked a fish of unimaginable magnitude. The only way he could haul it up was by reciting a chant to make heavy weights light.

When the great fish had at last reached the surface Maui left the canoe to find a priest who could make an offering to the gods and perform the appropriate ritual. He warned his brothers not to touch the mighty creature until this was done. The brothers, however, ignored him. They leapt from the canoe and began to scale the fish and to hack bits off it. The fish raised its fins and writhed in agony. The sun rose and made the flesh solid underfoot, its surface rough and mountainous because of the brothers' mutilation. It remained that way, and the name given to it was Te Ika-a-Maui, the fish of Maui.

The name for the South Island was drawn from its jade deposits: Te Wai Pounamu, greenstone water, or Te Waahi Pounamu, place of greenstone. The story of its origin told by the Ngai Tahu people was a variation of the creation myth. According to their account, Rangi the Sky Father had a union with Pohato-te-po before being joined with Papa. One of the children of this first marriage was Aorangi, rendered Aoraki in southern dialect. Aoraki and his brothers were opposed to the second marriage. In protest they left Hawaiki by canoe. In the vicinity of the South Island, however, their vessel struck a submerged reef and was wrecked. Aoraki and his brothers climbed to the higher side of the canoe so as not to drown. They waited so long for rescue that they turned to stone and became the Southern Alps. Aoraki or Mount Cook, the eldest, is the highest of the peaks; the others are the remaining brothers in descending order of seniority according to size. In this version, the Place of Greenstone is actually Te Waka-a-Aoraki, Aoraki's canoe. The Marlborough Sounds at the northern end represent the shattered prow, and Bluff Hill in the far south is the stern. The broken ranges of Southland and Otago are the jumbled remains of the vessel's cargo. Stewart Island (Rakiura) is the anchor stone.

Such mythology served the purpose for which it evolved. It gave meaning and continuity and therefore a measure of security to the lives of the earliest New Zealanders. Recounted, it conveys some of the textures of their collective imaginative life, their 'public dreams'. It offers clues to the manner in which they viewed the world and the puzzle of their existence in it. It is no substitute for what Western scholars understand by history, however, nor should it be confused with history.

The European writers at the turn of the twentieth century who converted Maori myths and legends into a chronological and so-called historical narrative took enormous liberties with the stories they used. They collected a number of migration traditions from different sources, merged them, transferred names from one to another, excised information that did not fit the pattern they created, and came up with an entirely new tradition – a Pakeha account of Maori history. Its basic outline was that New Zealand was first settled by a Melanesian race named Moriori, who were exterminated by the later Polynesian colonists. The country was discovered for the Maori and named Aotearoa by a navigator named Kupe in about AD 950. He was followed by Toi and Whatonga in about 1150, and they in turn were followed by a 'great fleet' migration of canoes in about 1350.

Examination of the nineteenth century sources for this account shows that there is no justification for believing the resulting story. There was a Kupe, but he was not first and he did not come in 950. Toi and Whatonga might also have lived, but not in the times and circumstances ascribed to them. There might well have been six canoes – and more – with the names assigned to them, but there is no evidence that they sailed together from some point outside New Zealand. Some of their individual stories are now thought to be figurative accounts of tribal migration within New Zealand. Oral traditions of this kind are important and they can reveal a great deal about the origins of tribal units, about inter-tribal relationships, about internal migrations, and about the bases for land claims. But they have to be read correctly. The major difficulty about using tribal traditions is that they are rarely simply accounts of what happened: they are selective attempts to explain and justify to the hapu things that have happened. They are frequently the stories of and the rationalisations of victors. They say little about the vanquished. They cannot and should not be used to provide absolute answers to objective questions such as who were the New Zealand Polynesians, where did they come from and how did they develop the characteristics that distinguish them from other peoples. Clues to these answers – and still only tentative ones – lie partially in tradition and far more in studies of linguistics, biological anthropology and archaeology.

The avid search among nineteenth-century scholars for the origin of the Polynesians is now known to have been an historical irrelevance. The Polynesians themselves never came from anywhere: their characteristics and their culture are now thought to have evolved in the central Pacific some two-and-a-half to three thousand years ago. The ancestors of these people, however, burst from the shores of South-East Asia and the South China Sea between four and five thousand years ago. Some went south-west, ultimately to Madagascar; others south-east along the Malaysian, Indonesian and Philippine chains. This much can be deduced from linguistic and archaeological features, and from the origins of the cultivated plants and domestic animals that these people carried with them into the Pacific.

What made these mighty journeys possible, indeed, what probably led to them, was the introduction of the sail to South-East Asia and the invention of the outrigger to stabilise craft on ocean voyages. Among the Austronesian languages shared by the people of the Pacific and the South-East Asian archipelagos the words for mast, sail, outrigger float and outrigger boom are among the most widespread and therefore among the oldest.

The Pacific Austronesians who made their way along the Melanesian chain of islands, reaching Fiji by 1200 BC and Tonga before 1100 BC, left behind fragments of pottery with distinctive decorations. It has been called Lapita after one of the places where it was found, and the same name has been given by archaeologists to the people who made it. With their pottery they also carried pigs, dogs, rats, fowls and cultivated plants. All these originated on the South-East Asian mainland with the exception of the kumara, which came from South America. (The latter proving that at some point Polynesians reached South America – where even the word for sweet potato is the same – and returned to the central Pacific; or that some South Americans travelled west into the Pacific. But the initial theory of Thor Heyerdahl that Polynesians originated in South America runs counter to all other evidence.)

A combination of excavation, radio-carbon dating and a study of language and adze forms has led scholars to the conclusion that Polynesian culture was generated by the Lapita people in the central

Pacific islands of Tonga, Samoa, Uvea and Futuna. Some have gone further and postulated that the Polynesian language developed in West Polynesia and the distinctive adze types in Samoa in particular. In addition, it is deduced that the Polynesian systems of kinship and social structure of aristocrats, commoners and slaves, and pervasive concepts such as mana and tapu, also evolved at this time.

Two further movements of Polynesians appear to have taken place in the last two millennia. Some sailed back to the west and settled the 'outlier' islands in the Melanesian chain, such as the Santa Cruz group, Tikopia and Rennell; others moved east again, peopling the Cooks, the Society and the Marquesas Islands. Here Polynesian culture was further differentiated and it was from this region that the eventual migrations to the farthest points of the Polynesian triangle were launched: to Hawaii in the north, Easter Island in the east and New Zealand in the south-west. The characteristics of early Eastern Polynesian culture, the earliest carbon dates and the subsequent rate of growth and spread of population all suggest that the New Zealand landfall was made before AD 1200.

The Pacific Ocean covers one-third of the globe. The area traversed by the Polynesians and their immediate ancestors is equal to that of China and the Soviet Union combined. Voyages of this magnitude have led to a debate among scholars as to whether they were deliberate or accidental. Did the Polynesians always set forth blindly into the unknown? Or did they move with some assurance in the direction of tiny land masses and — as they discovered them — move among them with a degree of deliberation and confidence? Traditional accounts speak of voyagers departing from one island or set of islands because of population pressure, or because of political or military defeat. There is little doubt also from traditional evidence that the Polynesians became adept at recognising the signs and locations of distant land in unexplored directions (cloud formations, for example, lagoon reflections, and — for far larger distances — the movements of migratory birds or the appearance of drifting vegetation on ocean currents).

With their twin-hulled or outrigger canoes and their considerable navigational resources Polynesians were able to make controlled journeys of hundreds and even thousands of kilometres. The navigational techniques included steering by stars, reading currents and swells and understanding how these were affected by contact with unseen land, use of the 'lapa' or underwater luminescence and awareness of the patterns of bird migration. The settlers who reached New Zealand – or at least those whose presence and descendants effectively colonised the country – are unlikely to have been simply blown off course on a voyage to somewhere else.

Computer analysis of wind and current movement and the imperatives of sailing techniques suggest that an accidental landfall was far less likely than a voyage of controlled navigation. There would have been signs (bird movements and floating debris) of a large land mass to the south of the central and eastern Polynesian islands. Further, to establish themselves in the manner they did, the colonising canoe or canoes would have had to carry men and women, cultivated vegetables, the Polynesian dog, the rat and a range of tools for practical use and for prototypes for those made subsequently from New Zealand materials. Bones of kiore or Polynesian rats in New Zealand have been dated at more than 2,000 years old – which could mean that the first human landfalls occurred even earlier than previously believed; but they may not have led to colonisation.

It is possible that an earlier exploratory discovery of the country was followed by a return journey to Eastern Polynesia, and that this led to a planned colonising expedition. Indeed, some of the discovery traditions assert that this is what transpired. Although some scholars have scoffed at the notion, the increasing information that comes to light about Polynesian navigation and recent successful experimental voyages demonstrate its probability. And excavations on Raoul Island – halfway between New Zealand and island Polynesia – uncovered New Zealand obsidian left there between AD 960 and 1360. This establishes at least one 'return journey'; the probability is that it was one of several. Further speculation awaits further evidence. And the only incontrovertible evidence of return voyaging would be the discovery of New Zealand materials on the islands of East Polynesia.

The land that the ancestors of the Maori found their way to more than 800 years ago was unlike anything that Polynesians had encountered elsewhere in the Pacific. As a fragment of the ancient super-continent of Gondwanaland it was far larger – more than 1,500 kilometres north to south – and more varied than islands colonised previously. It was temperate rather than tropical and sufficiently cold in much of the South Island to prevent the growing of crops. The three major islands had been formed by volcanic activity over 500 million years and much of the interior ruggedness reflected this former turbulence. Great wrinkles in the earth's crust had formed chains of mountains from the centre of the North Island to the Coromandel Peninsula, and from the East Cape down to the Southern Alps.

The land had largely settled by the time the Polynesians arrived, however, with the exception of the North Island plateau, Mount Taranaki and two offshore volcanic islands. Some people have speculated that it was the sight of one of these volcanoes – Whakaari or White Island – that gave the country one of its Maori names, Aotearoa, land of the long white cloud. This would suggest an initial landfall in the Bay of Plenty. The coastal lowlands were covered with broadleaf trees – pohutukawa in the north; karaka, ngaio and nikau; and in the south the southern rata. Inland, the forest was a mixture of broadleaf, podocarp and beech with a luxuriant bed of fern beneath. Some of the names given the trees, such as ni-kau (literally 'no coconut'), emphasise the origins and expectations of the earliest settlers.

Other than bats, there were no mammals ashore until the Polynesians released their rats (kiore) and dogs (kuri). It is possible that they also brought pigs and fowl with them but that these did not survive. This lack of meat was compensated for to some extent by the proliferation of seafood: fish, shellfish, crayfish, crab, seaweed, sea-egg and the sea mammals, whales, dolphins and seals. The forests contained fern root that provided a staple food when pounded, and there were more than 200 species of bird, many of them edible, some of them flightless. Inland waterways provided additional resources: waterfowl, eel, fish and more shellfish. To all these Polynesians added the cultivated vegetables they had brought with them – taro, kumara and yam, and the paper mulberry for cloth. For meat, in addition to fish and birds, there were limited supplies of dog and rat. Human flesh, a Maori anthropologist has noted, was eaten 'when procurable'.

The forest also offered larger trees than the first settlers had seen previously. With these they built bigger dugout canoes and evolved a complex tradition of carving. Later too they used wooden beams in the construction of houses. Materials such as raupo and nikau made excellent house walls and roofs. Flax plaited well into cords and baskets and provided fine fibre for garments. And there was an ample sufficiency of suitable stone materials for adzes, chisels and drill points, varieties of bone for fish-hooks, spear-heads and ornaments, and obsidian for flake knifes. Through these artifacts and crafts the New Zealand Polynesians developed one of the world's most sophisticated neolithic cultures. The land contained metals too, but these remained undiscovered.

Perhaps the most spectacular of the country's resources was the giant flightless bird, the moa, of which there were originally some twelve species. They ranged from the chicken-sized *Anomalopteryx* to the 3.7-metre-high *Dinornis gigantus*. They offered a food supply on a scale never before encountered in Polynesia (drumsticks the size of bullocks' legs) other than when whales were cast ashore. And some early groups of New Zealand Polynesians largely based their economy around them in areas where they were relatively plentiful until intensive exploitation drove the birds to (and perhaps caused) extinction.

The history of the first New Zealand colonists from the time of their arrival until the advent of Europeans is a history of their adaption to the environment just described – the matching of their skills and cultural resources to it, and the evolution of new features and emphases in their culture in response to the conditions that the environment imposed. Ethnologists now recognise at least two distinguishable but related phases of that culture. The first is New Zealand East Polynesian or Archaic, that displayed by the archaeological remains of the earliest settlers and their immediate descendants. The second is Classic Maori, the culture encountered and recorded by the earliest European navigators to reach the country. The process by which the first phase evolved into the second is a complex one, and one on which scholars are not yet in agreement. It is complicated by enormous contemporaneous regional variations in culture, and by the fact that in many regions quite different cultural trajectories occurred, resulting in considerable variation by the time of European contact.

What can be said with more confidence is that when James Cook and his men observed New Zealand Polynesians in the eighteenth century they had settled the land from the far north to Foveaux Strait in the south (although Cook himself, believing Stewart Island to be joined to the South Island, did not actually observe Maori in Foveaux Strait). The language these inhabitants shared was similar enough for one speaker to be understood anywhere else in the country, although dialectal differences were pronounced. And while other regional variations were apparent in the details and traditions of the culture, there were aspects of it that appeared to be practised by most of the population. Many of these were inheritances from or elaborations of earlier Eastern Polynesian features.

Competitive tribalism, for example, was the basis for what was later to be called Maori life. The family and the hapu (sub-tribe) were the units of society determining who married whom, where people lived, where and when they fought other people and why. Tribal ancestors were venerated along with departmental gods representing the natural elements. The whole of life was bound up in a unified vision in which every aspect of living was related to every other: art, religion, war, food gathering, love-making, death – all were an integrated part of a single fabric. And the universal acceptance of concepts such as tapu (sacredness or prohibition), mana (spiritual power, prestige), mauri (life force), wairua (spirit), hara (faults), utu (reciprocity) and a belief in makutu (sorcery) regulated these aspects of life.

Society was stratified, although not as rigidly as in some other Polynesian cultures such as Tonga and Samoa. People were born into rangatira or chiefly families or they were tutua (commoners); in practice, almost everybody could trace genealogical links to a rangatira line. They became slaves if captured in or as a consequence of battle. Immediate authority was exercised by kaumatua or older heads of families. Whole communities, sharing descent from an identified ancestor, were under the nominal jurisdiction of rangatira families whose authority was in part hereditary and based on the achievements of their forebears. In practice this authority had to be activated and reinforced by talent, performance and regard to the feelings of the kaumatua and followers. Occasionally federations of hapu and tribes would come together under a recognised ariki (paramount chief) for joint ventures such as making war or foraging for resources. The more common relationship among hapu, however, even closely related hapu, was competition mitigated by the cooperation of trading arrangements.

Communities ranging from a handful of households to over 500 lived in kainga or villages with a hapu base. Usually these were close to water and food sources, and to cultivations if the hapu possessed them. Sometimes the settlements were fortified, although fortifications were by no means universal. Most were in the North Island and dated later than AD 1500. More often villages were adjacent to a hilltop pa to which whole communities could retreat under threat. Where such pa existed they were elaborately constructed with an interior stronghold, ditches, banks and palisades. Some proved impregnable to siege; others were taken and lost several times in the course of a lifetime. Such defences were one of the features of Polynesian life that evolved in a more extensive and more complex manner in New Zealand than elsewhere in the Pacific. Some scholars speculate that the concept of the hilltop pa originated in the possession of kumara tubers and the need to protect them from marauders. Others see them as a result of increasing rivalry and as a visible statement of status.

Life was mostly organised around food gathering, food growing and (in areas where fighting was common) warfare. Cultivation was carried out communally, and foraging too was done in parties on a seasonal basis, to conserve supplies. When certain items were scarce or out of season they often had a rahui or prohibition laid on them by the community tohunga or priest. Warfare evolved as an important competitive element in Maori life in most (although not all) parts of the country. It was sometimes conducted to obtain territory with food or other natural resources (stone for tool making, for example); sometimes to avenge insults, real and imagined; sometimes to obtain satisfaction from hapu whose members had transgressed the social code; and sometimes as a result of disagreements about authority. One group that rejected warfare was the Moriori of the Chatham Islands, 870 km to the east of New Zealand. These people, descendants of early New Zealand Maori, outlawed group violence as a means of resolving disputes and focused instead on discussion or single-combat. They also evolved a more level society than Classic Maori and a modified language.

On the mainland, reasons for war were often flimsy and could be nurtured from generation to generation. The more important factor, perhaps, was that war or the threat of war kept successful communities and individuals alert, strong and resilient. It also brought about the annihilation of some hapu who did not display these qualities. For the most part, however, warfare was not totally destructive prior to the introduction of the musket. It was carried on more in the nature of competition for status. It often involved only individuals or small raiding parties, and ambush or sporadic attacks of short duration. Even when larger groups met in head-on confrontation or siege the dead rarely amounted to more than a few score. Most fighting occurred in summer months only and, except when an actual migration was under way, fighting away from a hapu's defined tribal territory was not common. For individual males as for tribes, the concept of mana was paramount; it was intensified and enlarged by the status of victor, diminished by that of vanquished. Courage and proficiency in combat were also vital ingredients in initiation and acceptance by male peers, especially in the case of rangatira who expected to exercise authority. The weapons most favoured were taiaha (long wooden-bladed swords) and short clubs, the latter most commonly called 'patu' or 'mere'.

Non-combatants were able to achieve high standing in the arts or in the exercise of esoteric powers as tohunga or chosen specialists ('chosen', it was believed, by the gods). Carving was highly prized and the working of wood, bone and stone in New Zealand reached heights of intricacy and delicacy seldom seen elsewhere. The best of the work in wood was to be seen on door lintels, house gables and canoe prows, and in stone and bone in personal ornaments such as tiki, pendants and necklace units. New Zealand jade or greenstone was especially valued for this latter purpose, and for fashioning into fine carving chisels. Like other Polynesians the New Zealanders had no access to metals prior to the eighteenth century.

Personal decoration in the form of moko or tattooing was also a feature of Maori art. Men were marked primarily on the face and buttocks, women largely on the face and breasts (exclusively chin tattooing on females is thought to have been a post-European development). Only in the Marquesas Islands did such decoration achieve comparable intricacy, with patterns apparent in both positive and negative aspects – a factor strengthening the case for the New Zealand link with East Polynesia. The Maori practice of the art was distinguished by the use of a straight blade in preference to a serrated chisel. This served not only to inject pigment into the skin, it also left a grooved scar which was more like carving in appearance than tattooing in other parts of the world.

In spite of competition, warfare and regional and tribal demarcations among the New Zealand Polynesians, trading was also extensive. South Islanders exported greenstone to other parts of the country for use in patu, adzes, chisels and ornaments. Bay of Plenty settlers distributed a high-quality obsidian from Mayor Island for flake knives. Nelson and D'Urville Island inhabitants quarried and distributed argillite. Food that was readily available in some districts but not in others, such as titi (mutton birds) from the far south, was also preserved and bartered. People were prepared and able to travel long distances for materials and food. And although ocean-going canoes appear to have disappeared from New Zealand by the eighteenth century – possibly because climatic changes had caused sea conditions to deteriorate – canoes were still used extensively for river, lake and coastal transport in the course of trade or war. Some of these craft were impressively decorated.

The gauze of romance that fictional and some ethnological accounts later threw over New Zealand Polynesian life was misleading. In many of its aspects that life was brutish and short. There was always the danger (for men, women *and* children) of being tortured or killed as a result of warfare. There was some ritual cannibalism. There was the possibility of disinheritance and enslavement in defeat. Further, medical examination of pre-European remains reveals that the natural life span was unlikely to exceed 30 years. From the late twenties most people would have been suffering considerably as a consequence of arthritis, and from infected gums and loss of teeth brought about by the staple fern root diet. Many of the healthy-looking 'elderly' men whose condition Cook commended at Queen Charlotte Sound in 1770 may have been, at the most, around 40 years of age.

There were many elements of life that New Zealand Polynesians shared, from the Aupouri people in the north to the Ngati Mamoe of the far south; a basic language, religious concepts, competitiveness, conventions of warfare, ways of giving and receiving hospitality. But it has to be stressed that the tribal basis of life and the size of the country had generated innumerable local variations. Settlements varied in size, construction, materials and layout; legends altered from district to district and incorporated local geographical features; dialects had evolved; some tribes tattooed extensively, others not at all; clothing varied according to location and climate, as did the patterns of food gathering.

Such were the contours of life that James Cook and other European navigators encountered towards the end of the eighteenth century in the people they called New Zealanders, and who later (from the middle of the nineteenth century) began to call themselves Maori. Their numbers were then around 100,000. They had no concept of culture as such, nor of nationhood or even race. They were tribal beings who were fiercely assertive of the identity that they found in their hapu membership. Their links to other Polynesians to whom they were related were almost as tenuous as those to the Europeans soon to invade their land.

CHAPTER TWO

TANGATA TIRITI

THE COMING OF PAKEHA

The first known contact between New Zealand Polynesians and Europeans was not auspicious. Abel Tasman anchored in Golden Bay in December 1642, warned by his principals in the Dutch East India Company that 'barbarian men are nowise to be trusted'. In the thickening dusk his crew exchanged shouts with brown men in canoes, and neither understood the other in the slightest. When the New Zealanders blew pukaea or war trumpets at the Dutchmen, Tasman had two of his own trumpeters play in reply. In effect a Polynesian challenge to fight had been issued and accepted. The outcome was inevitable. The following day four of Tasman's company were killed by the New Zealanders when they attempted to row from one of their vessels to the other. Ignorant of how this had come about the navigator condemned an 'outrageous and detestable crime', named the region Murderers' Bay, and then departed without setting foot on New Zealand soil.

Nearly 130 years later the English explorer James Cook displayed a more comprehending regard for New Zealand's inhabitants. His instructions about native populations differed from those given Tasman. The Earl of Morton, president of the Royal Society, had written that such people were 'human creatures, the work of the same omnipotent Author, equally under his care with the most polished European... No European Nation has the right to occupy any part of their country, or settle among them without their voluntary consent.'

Cook too was attacked. But he did not use such incidents as grounds for either departure or excessive retaliation. After only a fortnight on the New Zealand coast he noted shrewdly that a canoe-load of aggressors had dropped astern after the Englishmen had fired over their heads. 'Not I believe at all frightened... but content with having showed their courage by twice insulting us. We now begin to know these people and are much less afraid...' Cook recognised the bravado that was an inherent element in the New Zealanders' competitiveness and capacity for survival — the propensity for taking the offensive in uncertain situations so as to encourage themselves, discourage a potential adversary, and hence to make their own survival more likely. It was a long-established code of behaviour. After such exchanges, assured both of their own courage and their safety, the New Zealanders were often willing to barter and to offer friendship.

These early encounters contained the seeds for future patterns of race relations in New Zealand. In most respects other than in techno-logical development and knowledge of the wider world, New Zealand Polynesians were more than a match for Europeans. They were lively, curious, adaptable, potentially strong allies. But they were also (in subsequent European eyes) inconsistent, unreliable and even treach-erous. This was largely because their vivacity and versatility were matched to a vastly different set of preconceptions and values than those held by Europeans. Maori would take up many of the gifts offered by the evangelists of Western culture such as literacy, Christianity and agricultural and pastoral techniques. They would experiment with them and turn them to Maori purposes, determined by Polynesian concepts of relevance. If these tools did not then meet Maori expectations, they were likely to be discarded; if they did, they would be used in distinc-tively Maori ways. Maori were to take up with gusto the business of selling land, for example, only to find in many instances that their understanding of what had taken place in land transactions was very different from that of the Europeans involved.

It was the inability of most Europeans to distinguish between Maori and European expectations in this process — or to even admit the existence or validity of Maori expectations — that led to most of the difficulties between the races in the nineteenth century.

In the course of three visits between 1769 and 1777 Cook's relations with the New Zealanders were as cordial and mutually respectful as he could make them. There were misunderstandings, there were shootings in the course of attacks, kidnappings and thefts, and in 1773 ten of his men were killed and eaten on Arapawa Island. But the English navigator acted at most times with restraint and common sense (which he did not do in Hawaii in 1779, in the circumstances that led to his death). The presence of Tahitians on two of his voyages permitted the collection of a considerable body of material about the New Zealand Polynesians including information on language and on the nature of their culture, much of it volunteered by the New Zealanders themselves.

Cook was followed closely in 1769 by the Frenchman Jean de Surville, who sighted the country only two months later and passed within 50 miles of the Englishman during a storm off the northern coast. A second Frenchman, Marion du Fresne, visited the Bay of Islands in 1772 and was killed by New Zealanders as a result of some inadvertent transgression against custom there. His second-in-command, Julien Crozet, levelled the village concerned and massacred some 250 inhabitants in retaliation.

New Zealand was now — literally and figuratively — on the map. Consequently it was increasingly on the routes of European and North American vessels. But from the 1790s those vessels brought sealers, whalers and traders rather than explorers. The whalers began calling in 1791, the sealers the following year. Initially it was the latter who were more important. They concentrated their activities in the south, from the Otago coast around to Dusky Sound. Gangs were left by ships at camps for months at a time to slaughter the sea mammals in their thousands. Then the sealers would be collected with their cargo of skins and moved on to other locations or returned to New South Wales. The period of most intensive sealing was the decade up to 1810. From that year the focus of activity shifted to the sub-Antarctic islands.

Whaling affected New Zealand and New Zealanders over a far

longer period. Deep-sea whaling ships called regularly into Kororareka in the Bay of Islands for supplies, alcohol and women from the early 1790s. A number of Maori joined crews and spent some years at sea, travelling to Australia, other parts of the Pacific and even to North America. Shore-based whaling took over from the 1820s. Stations were established in Cook Strait, Banks Peninsula, Otago and the Chatham Islands. Others were set up on the Taranaki and Hawke's Bay coasts. Almost all these stations were close to Maori communities and relied heavily on them for food and other supplies. Because whaling was seasonal, most stations organised subsistence agricultural activities to support whalers at other times of the year. Inevitably whalers began to marry Maori women and Maori of both sexes worked in the settlements that grew up around the stations.

While sealers did encounter Maori (especially in Foveaux Strait), bartered with them and occasionally fought with them, it was the whalers who had the first significant effect on the lives of Polynesian New Zealanders. In the Bay of Islands crops were grown specifically for trade with European ships, additional slaves were acquired by local chiefs for labour and prostitution, and alcohol became readily available. In addition Maori there began to acquire metal tools and European clothing (and, slowly, muskets).

Europeans at shore whaling stations, especially those who had taken Maori wives and begun to raise families, became part of local tribal life. They too introduced tools, utensils and European garments to their districts. But the mores that dominated such communities remained Maori rather than European. The country still belonged to Maori, Maori were numerically dominant, and the European presence, in spite of the potential force of firearms, depended on Maori goodwill. Away from these places, especially inland, Europeans had little effect on Maori life at this time other than being indirectly responsible for the gradual spread of muskets and diseases.

Other vessels touched on the New Zealand coast for timber and flax and a regular trade grew up in both from the 1820s. Until the 1830s the influences of such trade on Maori tended to be apparent only in those places where Maori were involved or were providing supplies: in the Bay of Islands, Hokianga, Whangaroa, Mahurangi, Thames, Mercury Bay, Maketu. Such contacts gave Maori access to European goods, tools and clothing, and added grain and vegetables to traditional Maori crops – barley, oats, peas, maize, wheat, potatoes, pumpkin – and fruit. By the 1830s, usually with the assistance of missionaries, Maori were exporting many of these to New South Wales (and later still to California). As in the case of the whalers, European influences were strongest where traders settled and married Maori; but again, the mores of such settlements (that of Philip Tapsell at Maketu, for example) were Maori rather than European.

Inevitably, missionaries followed. Samuel Marsden of the Anglican Church Missionary Society was the first to visit in 1814. He was followed by the Wesleyans in 1822 and the Catholics (from France) in 1838. Proselytising did not begin in earnest until the 1820s. Like Europeans before them missionaries tended to settle in or close to existing Maori communities. Unlike their predecessors they wanted to change Maori life (by 'civilising' the New Zealanders) and they did not normally take Maori wives or lovers. Their influence at first was minimal. When it did become apparent it was more in the creation of a Maori interest in literacy and the growth of Maori expertise in agriculture than in conversion to a Christian church.

These effects were at first felt in the far north of the country where all denominations began their missions. As Ngapuhi Maori gradually came under Christian influence and began to release their considerable number of slaves in the 1830s, it was Maori evangelists so freed who began to carry the gospel to most southern parts of the country. These men had advantages over European missionaries, of course; they knew the country they were moving through, they spoke the language fluently, and they were known in their own tribal and hapu districts. When missionaries themselves eventually reached other parts of the country in the 1830s and 1840s, they frequently found their potential congregations familiar with the Christian message (although the Old Testament often appealed more than the New). And in some cases such groups already had Maori Bibles and prayerbooks, printed in the Bay of Islands from 1827, and many of them held services on the Sabbath as a matter of course.

The missionaries themselves began to record conversions and baptisms in the north from the late 1820s. Frequently these proved to be impermanent. Maori would often take from Christianity what seemed to fit their own needs and value structure and discard the rest. The Papahurihia movement which began in the north in the early 1830s, for example, was the first of many such 'Maori' religions. In these the adherents identified strongly with the Israelites of the Old Testament as a disinherited but chosen people promised deliverance and fulfilment by God. Such movements blended Biblical ingredients with Maori. They represented an acceptance by Maori of belief in Te Atua, the God of the Bible. But they were very much a Maori path to that God and a rejection of missionary insistence on Westernisation along with conversion.

The most dramatic early effect of the European presence in New Zealand, however, was the introduction and eventual widespread use of the musket. The acquisition of these weapons by the New Zealanders began in the 1790s as a consequence of the demand for timber and flax. In the Bay of Islands in particular traders were only too willing to barter guns for these commodities. Maori in turn were only too willing to acquire them – they revolutionised the shooting of birds – and it was only a matter of time before their value in battle became apparent.

The first recorded use of muskets in tribal warfare was at Moremonui near Manganui in 1807, when an armed raiding party of Hokianga Ngapuhi were intercepted by Ngati Whatua. In this instance both the use of guns by Ngapuhi and the outcome were indecisive. Over the next seven years muskets continued to be used in skirmishes among Ngapuhi and between Ngapuhi and Ngati Whatua of Kaipara, but they were present in limited numbers and tended to be used in hand-to-hand fashion, in the manner of traditional weapons, and so were not the cause of carnage.

The situation changed in 1814, however. Ngapuhi began a series of raids to the south – to the Coromandel Peninsula, Bay of Plenty, East Coast, Taranaki and the central North Island. They set out to avenge old scores, to acquire slaves, and ultimately to obtain flax, cloaks and smoked heads to trade for additional weapons. By now they were relatively heavily armed, some 30 or 40 muskets among about 400 men, and they used them with devastating effect. Musketless defenders sent out their best fighters to protect their pa from the first onslaughts only to see them incapacitated or killed by gunfire. The invaders would then finish off the survivors with hand-to-hand fighting. The scale of attacks from the north increased after the chief Hongi Hika visited England and Australia in 1820 and 1821. He returned with over 1,000 muskets and set off south again with more than 2,000 men. At the Mokoia and Mauinaina pa on the Auckland isthmus he built towers and fired at the defenders over their fortifications. Ngapuhi took both pa, slaughtered over 1,000 people and took many more back as slaves to work their flax cultivations.

The pattern changed as other tribes acquired muskets for defence, and then for aggressive expeditions of their own. Between 1810 and 1839 there were in all some 40 major armed raids touching all parts of the North Island except the King Country, and involving the northern half of the South Island. Of these, 30 were conducted by Ngapuhi, and the remainder by Waikato, Ngati Toa, Ngati Raukawa, Taranaki, Ngati Whatua, Ngati Tuwharetoa and Tuhoe. The Ngati Toa attacks on the Ngai Tahu and those of Taranaki on the Chatham Island Moriori in 1835 were especially devastating. Survivors also acquired muskets, however, and a new type of fortified pa evolved that was specifically designed for musket defence (flying buttresses allowed crossfire and there were shallow trenches for shooting out under palisades). A balance of weaponry if not of actual power was established, but at a terrible cost in human life. This was the major factor that brought such raids to an end in the late 1830s.

It did not mean the end of inter-tribal fighting, however. Skirmishes involving loss of life continued into the 1850s and 1860s. And tribal fighting was a major feature of the later New Zealand Wars as some groups joined up with the Imperial forces to carry on vendettas with traditional enemies, this time under the righteous banner of the British Crown.

Organised colonisation of New Zealand by Europeans began in earnest in the late 1830s. The Wakefield family's New Zealand Company took steps to establish settlements at Wellington, Nelson and New Plymouth. A French colony was set up at Akaroa on Banks Peninsula. Partly as a consequence of these private initiatives, and partly because of reports of appalling behaviour on the part of riff-raff Europeans in the Bay of Islands, the British Government decided to take steps to annex New Zealand. It hoped to do this with the consent of the native inhabitants. Indeed, protection of the New Zealand Polynesians from the alleged excesses of European behaviour and from the consequences of musket warfare was one of the primary reasons for the Government acting when it did. Captain William Hobson was dispatched to the Bay of Islands from New South Wales in 1840 as Lieutenant-Governor and, with the help of British Resident James Busby and CMS missionary Henry Williams, he drew up a treaty by which the New Zealanders themselves would cede sovereignty of their country to the British Crown.

Waitangi, the name of the estuarine river that runs below the site of James Busby's house on the west shore of the Bay of Islands, means 'waters of lamentation'. It would turn out to be an appropriate label to attach to the treaty signed in its vicinity in February 1840. For while that treaty was in part an outgrowth of the most benevolent instincts of British humanitarianism, and while those who signed it on 6 February had the highest possible hopes for benign outcomes, the document would turn out to be the most contentious and problematic ingredient in New Zealand's history.

The decision to annex New Zealand and the set of instructions drawn up for the man who would become its first governor, were deeply influenced by the evangelical religious beliefs of Colonial Office officials in the late 1830s. These men were part of the same movement which had agitated for and brought about an end to slavery in the

British Empire. Their concern for the welfare of Maori was genuine and profound. As time passed, however, and those same officials learned of the New Zealand Company's private-enterprise plan to colonise parts of New Zealand, then the emphasis of the office's plans changed. By 1839, as Claudia Orange has noted, the office was no longer contemplating a Maori New Zealand in which European settlers had somehow to be accommodated, but instead 'a settler New Zealand in which a place had to be kept for Maori'. Inevitably, Maori interests would suffer as a consequence of being moved down the priority list.

While Lord Normanby, Secretary of State for the Colonies, insisted that Hobson was to negotiate a willing transfer of sovereignty from Maori to the Crown, other problems would arise from the manner and speed with which the would-be Governor drafted the treaty to effect this transfer. Hobson was given no draft document prepared by lawyers or Colonial Office functionaries. Instead he had to cobble together his own treaty, with the help of his secretary James Freeman and British Resident James Busby, neither of whom were lawyers. That done, Hobson recognised that a treaty in English alone could hardly be understood, agreed to, or even debated by Maori, so he had the missionary Henry Williams and his son Edward hastily translate the English version into Maori. All this occurred over four days, with the Maori version being prepared overnight on 4 February.

On 5 February copies of the treaty in both languages were put before a gathering of Northern chiefs inside an enormous marquee on the lawn in front of Busby's house. There were hundreds of Maori present, Hobson's entourage of officials, English and French missionaries, and a solid phalanx of local Pakeha residents, who were not allowed to either debate or sign the document, which concerned Maori relations with the British Crown. Hobson read the treaty aloud in English, Henry Williams in Maori, and discussion between the proposers and the intended signatories followed. Because of his facility in Maori, it was inevitable that Williams spoke most often in defence of the treaty and its clauses when asked by Maori about meaning and implications.

In English, the preamble of the Treaty of Waitangi announced that

Queen Victoria regarded the 'Native Chiefs and Tribes of New Zealand' with favour and was 'anxious to protect their just Rights and Property and to secure to them the enjoyment of Peace and Good Order...' Because of this, and because of the continuing influx of British immigrants into the country, the Queen wished to 'appoint a functionary properly authorized to treat with the Aborigines of New Zealand [rendered in Maori as 'nga Tangata maori o Nu Tirani'] for the recognition of Her Majesty's Sovereign authority over... those islands...' The establishment of such authority would lead to 'a settled form of Civil Government with a view to avert the evil consequences which result from the absence of the necessary Laws and Institutions alike to the native population and to Her subjects...' To bring all this about, the 'confederated and independent Chiefs of New Zealand' – a deliberate echo of Busby's earlier Declaration of Independence – were invited to concur with three Articles and Conditions'.

The first article, and the key one for securing what was to follow, declared that the 'Chiefs of the Confederation of the Tribes of New Zealand', and those who have not become members of the confederation, 'cede to Her Majesty the Queen of England absolutely and without reservation all the rights and powers of Sovereignty... over their respective Territories...'

Under the second article in English, which in time would become the most contentious, the Queen guaranteed to the chiefs and tribes and their families 'the full exclusive and undisturbed possession of their Lands and Estates Forest Fisheries and other properties... so long as it is their wish and desire to retain the same in their possession'. At the same time the chiefs would give exclusive rights to the sale of land to the Queen and her representatives.

In the third article the Queen extended to the 'Natives of New Zealand Her royal protection and imparts to them all the Rights and Privileges of British Subjects'. A final clause noted that the chiefs, 'having been made fully to understand the Provisions of the foregoing Treaty', accept the spirit and the meaning of the document and attach their signatures and marks to it.

There was much in this document alone that would have been difficult to convey to members of a culture which did not share the same concepts, vocabulary and political and legal structures – especially the notion of sovereignty. These difficulties were compounded by the fact that the Maori translation of the treaty, the one most Maori would be addressing and debating and – if they thought they were in accord with it – signing, did not correspond to the English version in several key respects.

In the first place, the word used for sovereignty – that which the chiefs were asked to give away to the Queen of England – was rendered as 'kawanatanga'. Kawanatanga was an abstraction of the word kawana, governor, and hence meant literally 'governorship'. In the Declaration of Independence of the Chiefs of the Confederated Tribes, however, the word used for sovereignty had been 'mana', meaning 'authority over'. Critics of the treaty would thus be able to argue that the chiefs believed that they were retaining sovereignty, 'mana', and giving away only the right to 'governorship' of the country as a whole.

This impression would have been reinforced by the Maori wording of article two which assured them that they retained 'te tino ranga-tiratanga o ratou wenua kainga me o ratou taonga katoa' – meaning 'the unqualified exercise of their chieftainship over their lands, villages and all their treasures'. This was rather more than the same article offered in English: 'full exclusive and undisturbed possessions of their Lands and Estates Forests Fisheries and other properties...' Indeed, in future years, most Maori debate would focus on the implications of the words 'tino rangatiratanga', which some would claim was an even more accurate rendition of 'sovereignty' than mana; and they would argue that, in guaranteeing Maori tino rangatiratanga, the treaty was in fact guaranteeing Maori the right to continue to manage and govern their own affairs without interference of a civil or military authority.

Further confusion would arise over the article two term 'ratou taonga katoa'. In the English version this supposedly corresponded to 'other properties' which Maori would be allowed to retain; but in fact it was an expression with a far wider meaning, 'all their treasures'. It would be used in the future to argue Maori rights to material and cultural resources that were in no way envisaged by the English version or by those who proposed it.

None of these confusions were adequately addressed in the discussion that took place in the marquee on 5 February. On the contrary, missionary explanations of the terms and concepts, particularly those given by Henry Williams, fudged precise meanings and potential contradictions and emphasised instead the protective and benevolent intentions of the document as they would affect Maori. Clearly Hobson and his party and, apparently, all the missionaries with the exception of the printer William Colenso and the French Catholic Bishop Jean-Baptiste Pompallier, wanted the chiefs to sign as soon as possible and with a minimum of fuss. The majority of missionaries clearly believed that it was also in the interests of Maori, perhaps 'the only way that Maori could be saved from physical or spiritual extinction at the hands of the agents of vice', as James Belich put it.

No clear consensus was reached among the chiefs in the course of a five-hour discussion on the day of 5 February. Maori continued their deliberations late into the night on the river flat below Busby's house and lawn. The following morning 45 of them were ready to sign, and Hobson and his officials were summoned hurriedly to allow this to happen lest official dilatoriness provoked a change of Maori mind (the many paintings and tableaux which show Hobson in full Navy uniform serenely accepting Maori signatures is inaccurate; on the morning of 6 February he was garbed in a dressing gown).

Subsequent signings with local chiefs took place at Waimate North and the Hokianga in February, and later in nearly fifty other locations in the North and South Islands. Hobson proclaimed British sovereignty over the whole country on 21 May 1840, before the signings were complete, making New Zealand a dependency of New South Wales; and a year later New Zealand's own charter came into effect, making the country a separate colony of Great Britain.

While all these steps met internationally recognised constitutional procedures, there were loose ends that would constitute grounds for debate over the following 160 years: the fact that Hobson's proclamation of sovereignty preceded the collection of signatures; the fact that some chiefs of large tribes declined to sign the document or were not asked to; the fact that more than one English language version of the treaty was in circulation and subsequently signed; the fact that there were inherent contradictions between even the 'official' English and Maori versions; the fact that some Maori, with missionary encouragement, regarded the treaty as being in the nature of a 'sacred covenant', in the biblical sense, between themselves and Queen Victoria.

Almost 150 years later, when New Zealand governments tried to give judicial and moral effect to the document, they would seek to do so by defining yet another version, the 'spirit' or 'intent' of the treaty. This was a clear admission that the document itself, in all its manifestations and because of all its manifestations, was not a firm foundation for either the construction of a State or a blueprint for relations between governments and an indigenous people.

In 1840, however, the document served its original purpose. It enabled William Hobson, as the representative of the British Crown, to proclaim British sovereignty over the country and bring it into that family of nations known as the British Empire. Whether the treaty meant *more* than this at the time is debatable. Hobson would have been unable to govern the country, with a mere £4000, 39 officials and 11 'alcoholic' New South Wales police troopers, had not Maori given their consent. At any time Maori could withdraw their consent, as they did on various occasions in the 1840s and 1860s, and the civil and military authorities were unable to establish or fully regain control of those parts of the country where rebellions had occurred.

For the time being, however, the treaty offered Maori certain guarantees; many Maori had formed their own view of what those guarantees were and pronounced them acceptable. And the real object of the whole exercise, the British colonisation of New Zealand – with everything that implied by way of a transfer of people from one side of the globe to the other and an exploitation of the country's material resources for the benefit of both settlers and distant investors – was able to proceed. In the subsequent words of a Maori Land Court Judge, tangata whenua, the people of the land, would now be joined by 'tangata tiriti'; the people whose presence was authorised by the Treaty of Waitangi. And the face of New Zealand life would from that time on be a Janus one, representing at least two cultures and two heritages, and very often looking in two different directions.

Most Maori had welcomed European settlers when they had first encountered them. Because of the persistence of tribal competitiveness, chiefs saw Pakeha as a source of protection and a means of consolidating local power; they would be a source of muskets, trade goods and useful advice and a factor to enlarge the mana of the sponsoring chief and his hapu and kainga. Large-scale immigration in the 1840s brought a change in perspective, however. In 1830 there were just over 300 Europeans living in the whole of New Zealand. By 1840 there were about 2,000. And the Wakefield settlements (and the later ones in Canterbury and Otago) brought thousands more. The Ati Awa chief Wharepouri told Edward Jerningham Wakefield at Port Nicholson (later Wellington) that he had expected about ten Pakeha to settle there, one for each pa; when he saw the 1,000 who stepped off the first New Zealand Company ship at Petone, he panicked. It was beyond anything he had imagined; it seemed like an alien invasion.

Previously European settlement had taken place on Maori terms, with Maori in control of the process. Slowly Maori close to European coastal communities in the 1840s began to realise the extent to which their identity and customs could be swallowed by this mighty influx of foreigners. The Maori oratory of these years began to employ proverbs about the power of saltwater to contaminate freshwater (a nice metaphor this, because European flesh was reputed to taste markedly more salty than Maori); and the propensity of the kahawai for devouring the mullet.

Further, there was growing dissatisfaction over the manner in which land purchases were being carried out – by private buyers such as the Wakefields, and by Government officers. Sometimes only one faction of owners, whose claims might have been doubtful, were dealt with; others less malleable were ignored. Sometimes the goods or cash passed over in transaction were subsequently seen to be inadequate. And promises to set aside Native Reserves, even schools and hospitals in some areas, were not kept. Perhaps the most fertile seed for conflict in all this was mutual misunderstanding over what constituted land ownership. For European buyers it was a signed deed. For Maori it was a variety of factors including inherited rights, rights of conquest and rights of occupation and use. They sometimes refused to recognise the validity of sales that had been conducted with unauthorised persons, that were the result of trickery, or that had not resulted in subsequent occupation and settlement.

It was an instance of trickery that led to the first major clash of the New Zealand Wars, at Wairau in 1843. The Ngati Toa refused to recognise a fraudulent deed to land there held by Captain Arthur Wakefield for the New Zealand Company. When Nelson settlers including Wakefield attempted to clear the Maori off the land, fighting broke out. Twenty-two Europeans were killed, together with half a dozen Maori.

The Governor of the day, Robert FitzRoy (Commander of the *Beagle* on its epic scientific voyages from 1831–35), held that the greater blame for the 'massacre' (as it was termed) lay with the Nelson colonists. The anger of Wellington settlers at this verdict turned to fear as the Ngati Toa leaders at Wairau, Te Rauparaha and his nephew Te Rangihaeata, settled back on the northern side of Cook Strait, at Plimmerton and Pauatahanui. Over the next three years these chiefs became drawn into land disputes in the adjacent Hutt Valley. The tribes who had sold land around Wellington Harbour to the New Zealand Company, mainly Te Ati Awa, had settled the district under the patronage of the principal conquerors, Ngati Toa. And yet Te Ati Awa had not consulted Ngati Toa over the sales, and hence Ngati Toa did not recognise the validity of the transactions and participated in armed resistance to them. There were clashes at Taita, Boulcott's Farm, Pauatahanui and the Horokiri Valley. They ended with Governor George

Grey's arrest of Te Rauparaha, and Te Rangihaeata's withdrawal to Horowhenua. As an aftermath of this campaign there were further skirmishes in Wanganui in 1847 involving chiefs who had fought with Ngati Toa. But there were no further engagements in the lower part of the North Island.

While tensions had been mounting in Wellington even more extensive conflict had broken out in the far north. On 8 July 1844, the Bay of Islands Ngapuhi chief Hone Heke (or Ngapuhi acting for him) chopped down a flagstaff at Kororareka. Although he had been the first to sign the Treaty of Waitangi, Heke had become disenchanted with the effects of European colonisation. He believed the flying of the British flag deprived chiefs of their mana and Maori of their land. He announced his determination to remove this symbol of Maori subjugation and called on the Governor to raise a Maori flag in its place.

At first FitzRoy took no action other than to visit the area two months later, when most local chiefs expressed loyalty to him. On 10 January the following year, however, Heke cut down the new flagstaff. FitzRoy offered a reward for his capture and sent for more Imperial troops. Heke meanwhile gained the support of Kawiti, another powerful Ngapuhi leader, and together they attacked Kororareka on 10 March 1845. After one day's fighting (600 Maori against 250 armed defenders) they withdrew, leaving 13 Europeans dead and having lost somewhat more of their own fighters. In their wake a powder magazine exploded accidentally and set fire to much of the town. Maori and Pakeha joined in subsequent looting.

Two wars were waged in the months that followed, sometimes simultaneously, sometimes separately. Tamati Waka Nene and most of the Hokianga chiefs attacked Heke and his allies in a revival of earlier tribal conflict, and then these kupapa or 'friendly' Maori (meaning friendly to the British Crown) joined the Imperial forces for joint actions on Heke's and Kawiti's defended positions. The end came ten months later when Lieutenant-Colonel Henry Despard's troops breached Kawiti's pa at Ruapekapeka on a Sunday, after it had been deserted by the defenders. James Belich, in his major revisionist analysis of the New Zealand Wars, argues that – in every sense that mattered – Heke and Kawiti won the northern war. They were never defeated in any of its set-piece battles. Few of their men were killed (about 60 to the Imperial forces' 300). And they succeeded in tying up the British forces in exactly the way they had sought to. 'By building new pa in isolated locations, the Maori were able to channel military operations into economically unimportant areas. A British force attacking a new pa could not simultaneously attack Maori base areas. The resources used in such an expedition could not be used against other targets...'

The war had several important consequences. It was followed by thirteen years of peace nationally, apart from small-scale tribal skirmishes. Imperial troops developed a high regard for Maori skills in warfare. In particular, great admiration was expressed for the ingenuity of the fortified pa at Ohaewai and Ruapekapeka. In the space of about 30 years Maori had developed their strongholds from simple pa, to musket pa, to cannon pa, to virtual trench warfare. This evolution was noted by the Imperial forces. Major General Mould of the Royal Engineers made detailed reports on the construction of Maori rifle pits and trenches. The effect of these reports was to be seen in the use of trench warfare for the first time in Europe in the Crimea in 1853; and even more so in World War I when the use of the machine-gun made underground defences a necessity. Thus the inventiveness of Maori strategists contributed directly to the planning and conduct of international conflicts on the other side of the globe.

The decade that followed was, on the surface, one of peaceful interaction between Maori and Europeans. The modes of interaction differed in different parts of the country. Some Maori, of course, such as Tuhoe and Ngati Maniapoto, still saw virtually no Europeans other than itinerant missionaries. Others, such as the Waikato and Hauraki tribes, were expanding their crop production and supplying virtually the whole of Auckland's flour and vegetable requirements. Some hapu sold land willingly to the still-growing numbers of immigrants, often simply to assert the validity of their claims over those of competitors.

Others declined to do so and went so far as to form Land Leagues committed to no further sales. These latter were experiencing many of the misgivings about Maori survival first expressed in the 1840s. By 1860 the European population in New Zealand surpassed that of Maori for the first time, and it seemed to some chiefs that tribal culture and the mana of traditional Maori society would be entirely erased if steps were not taken to preserve them. And for some, a prerequisite for conservation was a ban on further land sales.

A series of meetings in the North Island in the 1850s canvassed the idea that Maori should unite under a king. This movement, inspired by Te Rauparaha's son Tamihana, arose in part from the fact that the presence of Europeans had created a sense of 'Maoriness' (and it was in this decade that the word Maori came into more common use by New Zealand Polynesians to describe themselves). It also arose from a belief that the key to apparent European superiority lay in their unity under the British Crown. If Maori could achieve a similar unity under their own monarch, it was argued, they would be able to match European confidence and cohesion, retain their lands and preserve customary law and traditional authority.

With these objectives in view the elderly and ailing Waikato chief Te Wherowhero was selected first Maori King in 1856 at a representative gathering of tribes at Pukawa near Taupo. He was installed in 1858 at his capital at Ngaruawahia and took the name Potatau. In the eyes of most European colonists this was an act of disloyalty to the British Crown, as was an expression of allegiance to a Maori monarch; in the eyes of Kingitanga supporters, the mana of the two monarchs would be complementary and serve different functions. Wiremu Tamihana of Ngati Haua, remembered as the Kingmaker, voiced this view at Potatau's raising-up ceremony: 'The Maori King and the Queen of England to be joined in accord; God to be over them both.'

The movement was viewed by Europeans as a blatant attempt to prevent land sales at a time when the towns of Auckland and New Plymouth were spilling over with colonists. Many settlers began to voice the opinion that only war could erase Maori disloyalty and open up land for further settlement. In this atmosphere war did indeed break out. Fighting began in Taranaki where Government officers had bought land from a minor Ati Awa chief not entitled to sell it. The owners occupied the block and resisted forceful attempts to remove them. Governor George Grey used Ngati Maniapoto participation in this conflict and an alleged threat to attack Auckland as an excuse to order the invasion of Waikato and the subjugation of the King Movement. Imperial and volunteer troops led by Lieutenant-General Duncan Cameron crossed the Mangatawhiri Stream in July 1863 and the Waikato War had begun.

It ended with the fall of Orakau nine months later, and two further battles at Tauranga. Six major engagements and dozens of skirmishes had caused over 1,000 Maori and 700 European casualties. It was followed by massive confiscations (1.3 million hectares) which further crippled and embittered the vanquished tribes. This latter action also secured for the New Zealand Government the land they had been seeking to reward their troops and to settle new colonists. The land taken was selected more for its fertility and strategic importance than for the owners' part in the so-called rebellion: some tribes who had remained loyal to the Government lost land along with those who had not; and the most bellicose group, Ngati Maniapoto, lost nothing. (The New Zealand Government showed little interest in the precipitous limestone hills and valleys of the King Country until it wanted to push the Main Trunk Railway through there in the 1880s.)

The New Zealand Wars were still not over, however. As the fighting in Waikato was winding down, a messianic movement that would generate further combat was gaining popularity in Taranaki. Pai Marire (known to Europeans as Hauhau) promised its followers deliverance from European domination. Its founder, Te Ua Haumene, identified closely with the Psalms of David and wove Biblical and Maori elements into a ritual that included incantation and dancing round a niu pole, a gigantic version of the traditional Maori divining stick. The movement also revived warrior traditions and the pre-European practice of ritually eating the hearts and eyes of slain victims. In the minds of its followers it was an emphatic rejection of the European ways advocated by missionaries; in the minds of Europeans it was barbaric and the choice of name utterly inappropriate (Pai Marire means 'good and peaceful').

From 1864 to 1868 government and Hauhau supporters fought sporadic skirmishes in Taranaki, the Bay of Plenty, the East Coast, Rotorua and Wanganui. The campaign also spawned a further one. After fighting at Waerenga-a-Hika near Gisborne in November 1865, a Maori on the government side who came to be known as Te Kooti Arikirangi Te Turuki was wrongfully arrested and deported to the penal settlement in the Chatham Islands. He broke out of there, commandeered a ship and returned to New Zealand to wage the most effective guerrilla campaign seen in the country. He was chased by kupapa and European troops through the East Coast, Urewera and central North Island for four years, and he finally withdrew to sanctuary in the King Country in 1872. Traditionally the last shots of the New Zealand Wars are regarded as those fired by Gilbert Mair's Flying Arawa Column at Te Kooti's retreating forces on 14 February 1872.

If the wars themselves were over by 1872, the threat of them was not. Pakeha were still forbidden to cross the Aukati Line into the King Country where the Maori King Tawhiao lived with his followers. Three Europeans who did so were slain. This chapter too came to an end when Tawhiao emerged from his exile in 1881 and laid down his arms before Major William Gilbert Mair, Resident Magistrate at Alexandra. This might have signalled the end of armed conflict, but it was not the end of tension.

Maori continued to be confused about the status of land supposedly Pakeha owned – as a result of sale or confiscation – but not occupied or used. In 1877 the prophet Te Maiharoa led a heke (migration) of Ngai Tahu from Temuka to the Upper Waitaki Valley, to reoccupy old tribal grazing land. Two years later the community he had established there was forcibly evicted by police. And in 1881 the Native Minister John Bryce led 1,300 troops into Parihaka Pa in Taranaki to destroy it and arrest dozens of the male inhabitants. This was in retaliation for a passive resistance campaign against the surveying of the Waimate Plains, uninhabited confiscated land which the Government intended to sell.

One further incident threatened the uneasy peace. In 1898 the Hokianga County Council, following a precedent set by other local bodies, imposed a ten shilling tax on all dogs in its territory. This was regarded as unfair by local Maori; they resented taxation of any kind when they did not receive amenities in return, they did not have a great deal of cash, and they owned on average far more dogs than Europeans. A group of dissenters from Te Mahurehure tribe gathered in the village of Waima and sent a message to the county office that they would shoot anyone who forced them to pay. The Government over-reacted and sent five ships to the area loaded with armed police and troops. A potentially explosive situation was averted by the Member of Parliament for Northern Maori, Hone Heke (grand-nephew of the 'axe-man'), who dashed to the area on horseback from Whangarei and persuaded the rebels to lay down their arms.

Thus ended the so-called Dog-tax War without a shot being fired. And so did the era and the climate that had produced the violence of the New Zealand Wars. From the late nineteenth century Pax Britannica was in effect over the whole country. When Maori took up arms in the future it was not in defence of tribal or even Maori interests; it was abroad on behalf of the whole country as members of national Expeditionary Forces.

CHAPTER THREE

TANGATA MAORI

being Maori

The Maori population declined sharply in the nineteenth century as a result of contact with Europeans. Polynesian genes had been separated from the continent of Asia for some 5,000 years, and therefore from continental diseases. Their bearers had no natural resistance to influenza, measles and whooping cough, and venereal disease and tuberculosis were previously unknown to them. Changes in living conditions also led to typhoid and dysentery in epidemic proportions. The precise extent to which such diseases, coupled with the casualties of the musket wars, reduced Maori numbers in the first half of the century is unclear because of uncertainties about the reliability of Maori statistics. Current demographic calculations suggest that the population at the time of Cook's visits was in the order of 100,000. In 1843 Ernst Dieffenbach travelled the country extensively, spoke to those who had travelled further, and estimated the native population to be nearly 115,000. That one or both early figures is incorrect seems likely; or the Maori population remained relatively stable from the 1770s to 1840s.

What is far more certain is that numbers did decline dramatically from the 1840s to the 1890s. Epidemics of influenza, measles and whooping cough were reported with some frequency in the 1840s and 1850s, as far more Maori than previously had contact – directly or indirectly – with Europeans; there were also dysenteric outbreaks of massive proportions over the same period. The fertility rate declined markedly as women suffered from general ill-health and from the effects of syphilis, gonorrhoea and tuberculosis. In parts of Waikato in the late 1850s over one-third of married Maori women were found to be barren. Communities visibly shrank in the face of these onslaughts: some Ngati Ruanui villages in Taranaki, for example, lost one-third of their populations as a result of death from illness between 1846 and 1852. Nationally the Maori population dropped from Dieffenbach's estimated 114,800 in 1843 to 56,049 in 1857–58, and to 42,113 in the 1896 census. As such figures became known they contributed to a widespread belief that the Maori people were headed towards extinction. Wellington Provincial Superintendent Dr Isaac Featherston echoed liberal European sentiment in the late nineteenth century when he spoke of the responsibility to 'smooth the pillow of a dying race'.

Conditions in Maori settlements varied enormously, however, from district to district – so much so that it is difficult to generalise about Maori life in the latter half of the nineteenth century. One reason, of course, is that the basis of this life remained hapu and tribe. Maori generally still did not view themselves as 'Maori' (that is, as a single race and culture) even after the word Maori had come into more common use. Consequently there was as yet little incentive for them to behave in a homogeneous way, other than to continue – in characteristically tribal manner – to disparage and to compete with Maori from other hapu and other places. The very persistence of tribal feeling had prevented the continuation of 'nationalist' experiments such as the Kingitanga. (Although the Maori King Movement survived the Waikato War, it did so as the almost exclusive preserve of the tribes of the *Tainui* waka federation: Waikato, Ngati Maniapoto, Ngati Haua, Hauraki. It had in effect ceased to be multi-tribal in the second half of the nineteenth century, although it was subsequently to become so again.)

Tribal feeling had prevented Maori from acting as a pressure group commensurate with their numbers. Even though four Maori seats were created in the national Parliament in 1867, tribalism and regionalism at first prevented its members from acting in concert from common Maori aims (as did the fact that some of the early members were not proficient in English, and few European members spoke Maori).

In spite of such diversity and divisiveness, most Europeans rarely distinguished one Maori from another or one tribe from another – a fact especially evident in cartoons of the Maori in the late nineteenth century. Maori were all simply 'Native' in the language of official usage; those of part-Maori descent were almost always identified exclusively with that side if their features or colouring were even slightly Polynesian in character. A European visiting a Maori settlement was very much aware that he was in a world different from his own. The dispositions of such communities, the provision of communal meeting, cooking and eating facilities, the style of houses, the materials from which they were built, the nature of the activities that went on in and around them, the language that was spoken, the kind of food that was eaten and the manner in which it was prepared, the general broadcasting of excreta – all these features suggested to Europeans a distinctively Maori lifestyle, and one that seemed indistinguishable from place to place.

Traditional Maori clothing had gone out of general use by the 1850s (and much earlier in communities involved in whaling and trading and those close to European settlements). As the settler population had swollen in the previous decade, so European clothing had become widely available, new and second-hand, along with blankets. Clothing and blankets were sold by travelling merchants and storekeepers who reaped excessive rewards in some areas, exploiting the market for both commodities. There was a simultaneous Maori demand from the same entrepreneurs for pipes, tobacco, axes, spades, cooking utensils (especially billies, camp ovens, kettles, buckets and knives), and for metal to make other tools.

Traditional garments made from flax, flax-type plants and dog skins had been time-consuming to prepare and had not provided satisfactory protection and warmth. Blankets were welcomed as a means of keeping warm at night without having to rely entirely on fires inside houses without chimneys, which had detrimental effects on eyesight and lungs. Blankets were also adopted widely as garments: typically one around the waist would serve as a skirt or kilt, one around the shoulders as a shawl; people also took to wearing them toga fashion, in imitation of traditional cloaks. As the century wore on traditional clothing – cloaks, waist mats, flax skirts and so on – came to be used exclusively as ceremonial costume. They would often be worn as part of haka and action-song performances or, in the case of cloaks, placed over European dress to emphasise the person's Maori identity or rank within the Maori community.

Generally in the nineteenth century Maori settlements continued to be built around hapu membership and they ranged in size from half a dozen households to several hundred. Each community was likely to have five kinds of building: whare mehana or sleeping houses; kauta or communal cookhouses; pataka or storehouses; whata or shelters for storing wood; and – with increasing frequency as the century drew near its close – wharepuni or community meeting houses. A whare mehana might shelter an immediate family (husband, wife and children) or an extended one. It would be used for sleeping and for the storage of personal possessions, rarely for cooking and eating, which would more commonly take place in community facilities. The size and style of these and other Maori constructions gradually changed with the availability of European tools, garments, utensils and other materials.

In the earlier years of the nineteenth century whare mehana were typically small (about 4.6 metres by 3.7), low (1.8 metres) with low doors and poor ventilation. Wooden houses often had earth heaped against the walls for further insulation; raupo ones, which became more common in the mid-nineteenth century, were free-standing. Usually they were warmed by small charcoal fires or embers spread on the floor, and lit with lamps made by floating wicks or charcoal in containers of fat. As European clothing spread and blankets became generally available, the houses became larger and better ventilated and were built above the ground. Chimneys and European-type fireplaces were being added in many districts from the 1870s.

Wharepuni or community sleeping houses increased greatly in size to the kinds of dimensions (18 to 24 metres long, 8 metres wide) that were to become common in the twentieth century. (There were no large permanent meeting houses in pre-European years, although temporary shelters of considerable length were not uncommon; the permanent meeting house became possible and desirable with the advent of European garments and tools, and with the increase in inter-tribal hui after the New Zealand Wars.)

The incentive for constructing larger community buildings was greatest where tribes had regular inter-hapu or inter-tribal meetings to sustain – such as Waikato with its Kingitanga hui (poukai) and Tuhoe with its Ringatu gatherings (tekaumarua). In general, observers noted in the 1870s and 1880s that large and lavishly catered meetings were becoming an increasingly common feature of Maori life since fighting was no longer available to provide excitement or a focus for community effort. The larger and more lavish the hui, the more mana accrued to the host community – prestige in Polynesian terms being measured by what was given away rather than by what was accumulated. Such gatherings required adequate accommodation and were a factor in the enlargement of meeting houses. Another factor was the availability of pit-sawn timber and European tools; the latter aided large-scale construction and the evolution of increasingly elaborate styles of carving, especially in Arawa territory. A knowledge of European architecture also modified the styles of smaller buildings in some areas, even where traditional materials were still in use; some dwellings, such as those in Tawhiao's settlement at Whatiwhatihoe, had doors at the side covered with verandahs.

In most districts traditional building materials – raupo, muka, ponga, earth sods, bark, nikau – continued to be used into the 1880s. Houses were likely to have wooden frames, usually of manuka or tree fern trunks, and wall material of reed or wood packed against them. Sod walls remained in favour in some South Island communities at this time – partly because wood was not always available and partly because they gave more adequate insulation from the colder climate. Roofs were thatched with reed, nikau or tussock, or they were covered with bark. Such structures were still visible in the early years of the twentieth century, although by then such use was in decline.

Generally, as pit-sawn timber and corrugated iron became available in the last two decades of the nineteenth century, Maori were quick to make use of them where they could afford them. House styles changed in the process. Important and wealthy people increasingly came to live in European-type houses, often indistinguishable externally from a rural Pakeha homestead. Other Maori tended to opt for simple rectangular huts and cottages with fireplaces and chimneys. Some leading subsistence lives combined European *and* Maori building materials. Te Puea Herangi of Waikato, for example, used ponga walls for conventional cottages into the 1930s and 1940s. While people engaged in seasonal work or foraging activities − flax cutting, gum digging and mutton birding, for example − continued to build traditional-type shelters and camp sites, these should not be confused with so-called substandard permanent housing.

In the nineteenth century most families slept in their whare mehana, worked with other families in communal cooking areas or kitchen shelters and stored food in common storehouses. With the advance of the twentieth century there was a tendency for individual family dwellings to be extended and to include cooking and eventually full kitchen facilities for day-to-day living. Cooking on a large scale for hui, however, would still be done communally, as would washing clothes (in rivers or portable tubs), harvesting communal crops and foraging for seafood and for wild vegetables such as puha and watercress.

In European eyes most Maori accommodation in the nineteenth and early twentieth century was decidedly substandard. Indeed, an absence of toilet facilities of any kind, a lack of running water, overcrowding in sleeping quarters, a lack of ventilation and generally unhygienic conditions for the preparation of food − all these features were to be characteristic of Maori communities and individual dwellings until the 1940s. 'Maori housing' in European usage was synonymous with poor housing. These features were the first to be criticised and then combated by Maori health authorities when they were appointed for the first time in the early 1900s. They were not obviously inimical to Maori lifestyles, however, and therefore there was little immediate incentive for communities to change them. Latrines tended to be built under the supervision of a visiting health officer and then abandoned when he left. But such conditions did contribute to the spread of tuberculosis, typhoid fever, dysentery, and diarrhoeal and respiratory diseases, and generally made outbreaks of any contagious illnesses more likely to affect whole communities. Inasmuch as sickness debilitated people or shortened their lives, then such conditions were a threat to the survival of Maori people and hence of Maori culture. And once Maori leaders had made such a cause-and-effect connection, they fought hard to change them, locally and nationally.

Some communities attempted to anaesthetise themselves from health problems and from grief from resulting deaths with excessive use of alcohol – with the result that their members became even more susceptible to ill-health and less capable of coping with the crises that illness brought. In this way whole villages and hapu in some areas were prone to sink into sloughs of despondency from which it was difficult to emerge. Te Uira Te Heuheu, a Tuwharetoa woman who married into such a community in Waikato in 1913, was shocked. 'There seemed to be no sense of direction,' she wrote later. 'Life just drifted by.' (Her shock, it should be noted, arose from the fact that such conditions were by no means universal; some Maori communities, especially those with a sound economic base on the East Coast of the North Island, in Hawke's Bay and in parts of the South Island, were coping with their vicissitudes with determination and considerable success.)

For a long time the official attitude to problems of Maori health and welfare was to ignore them. There were, in effect, two New Zealands: Pakeha New Zealand, served and serviced by comprehensive systems of national and local government administration; and Maori New Zealand, largely ignored by both except when those systems wanted to appropriate resources such as land, income or manpower. Maori were unable to obtain housing finance until the 1930s. Few doctors saw Maori patients, hospitals rarely took them and most did not want to. The Auckland Health Officer – in whose district lived the bulk of the country's Maori population – stated in 1911 that Maori health should be of concern to Europeans; but only because the unchecked spread of Maori diseases could lead eventually to Europeans contracting them. 'As matters stand,' he wrote, 'the Native race is a menace to the well-being of the European.'

In spite of these fears of contamination, the Maori population was well insulated from the non-Maori throughout the nineteenth century and for the first half of the twentieth. In 1900 more than 95 percent lived in rural communities that were so scattered as to cause not only geographic separation of Maori from Pakeha, but also separation of Maori from Maori. The major concentrations were north of Whangarei, in South Auckland, Waikato, the King Country, the Bay of Plenty, the East Coast, Rangitikei, Wanganui and Taranaki. Families continued to live for the most part in kainga with a hapu base or, in more isolated districts, in individual family homes outside kainga. The South Island Maori population, which numbered only 1,400 in 1901 out of a national total of 45,000, lived in half a dozen major kaika or 'kaiks' (renditions of 'kainga' in South Island dialect) close to but separate from European settlements in Canterbury, Otago and Westland.

Life for people in such settlements tended to be family-, community- and hapu-oriented. On occasions this orientation would extend to wider tribal units, especially when land matters were discussed or disputed; or to a waka federation such as Tainui or Mataatua. This latter was especially likely where wider organisations such as the Kingitanga and the Hahi Ringatu activated more extensive relationships and obligations on a regular basis. Effective leaders were the kaumatua or family heads, while whole hapu would be spoken for at wider hui by rangatira who usually had a whakapapa claim to leadership, but whose tenure also depended on retaining the confidence of their kaumatua.

Major decision-making on community matters was centred on consensus-forming discussion among family heads on local marae. In the South Island, kaika had established runanga in which whole com-munities were likely to be involved, and which would be chaired and spoken for by upoko runanga or community heads. In rare cases, such as Waikato-Maniapoto and Ngati Tuwharetoa, ariki or paramount chiefs would speak for federations of tribes; more often, as in the case of the Ngai Tahu/Ngati Mamoe land claim in the South Island, tribal spokesmen would be rangatira dominant at a particular time or nominated by the rest of the tribe to represent them for a particular project. Within these defined but flexible structures communities organised their rounds of hui, tangi and church functions, arranged marriages to strengthen useful alliances among families and hapu, planned, constructed and maintained community facilities such as meeting houses and dining halls, dealt with local conflict and often resolved it, and discussed the perennial issues raised by prospects of land sales or public works in the vicinity of the kainga.

A few Maori communities were for a time spectacularly and successfully self-reliant, sustaining their inhabitants and protecting them from the effects of disease, alcohol and demoralisation. Te Whiti O Rongomai's pa at Parihaka, with its Taranaki tribal base, was one such successful experiment. From the late 1880s it had its own slaughterhouse, bakery, bank and prison, and it generated its own electricity for lighting. A similar experiment in Maori independence which made use of European technology was launched by the prophet Rua Kenana in the Urewera in the early 1900s. Other pa, such as Whatiwhatihoe in the King Country and (in the 1890s) Waahi near Huntly, were not as well equipped in Pakeha technology as Parihaka and Maungapohatu, but they were able to nourish their inhabitants and to provide lavish accommodation and hospitality for visitors, Maori and Pakeha. Some, like those in the South Island, close to European centres of population and mingling with Pakeha in work and sport, were by the beginning of the twentieth century almost indistinguishable in external appearance from a Pakeha village. Others such as the smaller Tuhoe settlements in the Urewera had changed very little in appearance since the wars of the 1860s. In these as in other respects, Maori life was characterised by diversity.

(The Urewera was the last Maori district to be 'penetrated' by Europeans, and for this reason it became a popular target for ethnologists. These men, most interested in manifestations of the 'old-time' Maori, tended to ignore or condemn the experiment in acculturation being conducted by the Tuhoe spiritual leader Rua Kenana.)

Most of these communities made a precarious living from mixed subsistence farming. The scale of Maori horticulture had diminished greatly from the days of the 1840s and 1850s when the Waikato, Hauraki, Arawa and Bay of Plenty tribes had been the country's major crop producers and exporters. Later in the century, with most of their good land bought or taken from them, denied access to the government assistance given Pakeha farmers for land development, Maori in most parts of the country could barely produce sufficient meat, grain, vegetables and fruit to feed themselves. In some places – the Urewera, for example – communities lived close to starvation. In other areas, such as Maketu in the Bay of Plenty, Maori labour and produce were plentiful.

Where families and communities were unable to be self-sufficient – and this was the case in the majority of Maori settlements – Maori labourers came to rely increasingly for income on seasonal work created by the expanding European rural economy. It was common for Maori gangs in rural districts to take up fencing, drain laying, shearing, crop harvesting, flax cutting and processing, scrub cutting, timber felling and gum digging, or road and railway public works. Often whole families or hapu would specialise in specific jobs. In many areas such work was available from Pakeha farmers or local bodies adjacent to hapu settlements. Where individuals left their own kainga in search of such work they tended to settle in other rural Maori communities, adopting the identity and kawa of their hosts, or of the family and hapu into which they married. This served to mitigate the appearance and effects of detribalisation which – while it was under way from the early years of the twentieth century – did not become dramatically apparent for another generation as a result of migration for work and the demise of small communities through depopulation.

The commitment to Maori values remained strong, in spite of the fact that most Maori had been nominally converted to Christianity (the largest number to the Church of England; the rest to Roman Catholicism, Methodism, Mormonism and Presbyterianism, in that order). Mana and tapu were still decisive factors, determining who led communities, who deserved respect, and what was or was not done. It was still widely believed that hara or 'faults' in a Maori sense created chinks in an individual's personal tapu, and that this in turn left the individual vulnerable to makutu, sickness, madness or death; most instances of actual sickness or death were explained in these terms. Tohunga continued to perform Maori karakia or religious rites and to practise folk medicine, sometimes with disastrous results when dealing with 'Pakeha' illnesses such as measles or influenza (immersion in water was a common feature of Maori ritual).

In some areas Maori were 'Christian' in some contexts – a wedding or church service, for example – and 'Maori' in others, such as combating makutu or performing ritual prior to planting crops or felling trees. Some people practised Christian and Maori religions simultaneously: most Waikato Maori under the Kingitanga, for example, were followers of Pai Marire and baptised Methodists. This was not seen as contradictory. Maori increasingly came to view life in terms of taha Maori and taha Pakeha – the Maori and the Pakeha sides of themselves and of the world in general.

Increasingly, the focal point of Maori life was the hui. People who could no longer fight one another came together to compete in other ways: to surpass the hospitality of their previous hosts and put them back in debt; to issue oratorical challenges and display astonishing feats of memory in the recitation of genealogy and tradition; to debate other people's versions of genealogy and tradition; to display prowess in haka, action song, wielding the taiaha and handling canoes.

The hui was an established Maori institution throughout the country. The Ngai Tahu of the South Island restored their tribal identity by meeting regularly and debating how to act in concert to prosecute their land claim. The people of the Wanganui and King Country met to debate Native Land Court questions, where the Main Trunk Railway should be allowed to go, where roads could be laid, and the extent to which Maori communities should be relocated to take advantage of these new arteries of communication. Ngati Kahungunu hapu met to discuss the Repudiation Movement which challenged Pakeha land purchases in Hawke's Bay. Tuhoe met to debate whether they should allow surveying and gold prospecting in the Urewera. Waikato tribes came together interminably to discuss new proposals for Maori political representation, the mana of the Kingitanga and the sale and leasing of land.

But in a sense these were simply excuses for, not causes of, hui.

Essentially hui were occasions on which hapu could come together in wider tribal units, to renew old relationships, to sing, to dance, to tell stories, to argue in and listen to lengthy whaikorero. More and more in the latter years of the nineteenth century these hui were becoming inter-tribal ventures as leaders and followers felt impelled to debate the great questions of the day. By the 1890s a feeling was growing among some leaders that a form of 'Maori' rather than specifically tribal political activity should be attempted to promote common Maori causes, particularly in dealings with the national Parliament.

All such meetings were conducted according to Maori kawa, though the details of such etiquette varied slightly from tribe to tribe and from district to district. In some the hosts spoke first, in others the visitors, in some hosts and visitors alternated speakers, in others they followed one another until each group finished separately; most tribes forbade women speaking on the marae, some tolerated it, a few encouraged it; all these things had evolved and become fixed in the years that tribes were separated from one another. The general structure was similar throughout the country, however. Successive waves of visitors would be called on to the host marae, they would pause to tangi for the dead of both sides, they would be greeted by speeches and waiata that asserted the identity of the hosts and they would reply in kind with their own speeches and songs, they would hongi with the hosts to indicate that the tapu of visitor status had been removed through the ritual of welcome, and then they would be fed.

The hui ritual that remained strongest, and which some called the heartbeat of Maori culture, was the tangihanga or ceremony of mourning for the dead. This practice was modified slightly over the years to incorporate some Christian elements and to meet public health requirements. But basically its sequence and effect did not change from the nineteenth to the twentieth centuries. When a person died the body was laid out on the marae of the family or hapu. It was exposed to view (at first on mats and blankets, later in open coffins) for days while mourners came to pay respects and to comfort the bereaved. The tupapaku (corpse) was addressed in oratory and lament, as were the spirits of the relatives who had predeceased him or her. Fine mats, cloaks and tribal heirlooms were also on display, to demonstrate the mana of the hapu and to symbolically warm and protect the deceased. From the 1890s photographs were incorporated into the ritual to recall the presence of the dead. At about the same time portraits also began to be placed on meeting house walls, an extension of the concept which regarded such houses as representations of the genealogy of the hapu.

The duration of tangi varied. Until the end of the nineteenth century they could go on for weeks, even months if the deceased was sufficiently important (the last one of considerable length was that for King Tawhiao in 1894, which lasted nearly two months). Public health legislation early in the twentieth century restricted the mourning time and it became customary to hold ceremonies within the space of one week; improving systems of transport and communication also reduced the need to display the body for longer periods. The ceremonies ended with a Christian funeral service, usually conducted by a Maori minister, and a European-type burial in which many of the deceased's personal possessions were likely to be interred with the body. A year or more later another ceremony would be held to 'unveil' the headstone, and this fulfilled some of the functions of the pre-European hahunga or exhumation rite, which ended the period of mourning. Late in the nineteenth century Maori women began to wear black clothes for tangi, and the practice continued in many areas long after Europeans in New Zealand had stopped wearing mourning garments.

Although the proceedings of the country's Parliament were remote from the daily lives of most Maori, some legislation had intimately affected them. Since European settlers had been granted so-called Responsible Government by the British Parliament in the 1850s and 1860s, one of the greatest difficulties had been devising ways to ascertain ownership of Maori communal land and hence who to deal with in sales transactions. The problem increased as the European population in New Zealand increased. Inevitably too, Pakeha buyers wanted the best agricultural and pastoral land available. In an attempt to accelerate such transactions the Native Land Court was established in 1865, its functions superseding many of those of the earlier Native Land Purchase Department. This later institution held sittings presided over by a judge to investigate claims to land, to rule on the validity of such claims, and to record the names of successful claimants as owners. Although the court was undoubtedly intended to facilitate the transfer of Maori land to Pakeha ownership, Maori themselves showed a considerable willingness to bring land to the court and often to offer such land for sale. The reasons for this were complex. In some cases owners simply wanted money with which to purchase other commodities, in some instances the land concerned was not wanted, but in many cases court sittings and sales seem to have been initiated by Maori simply to prove the validity of their claims over those of rival Maori. The sittings became, in other words, another forum for the inter-hapu and tribal rivalries that had always characterised Maori life. In many instances spurious claimants launched proceedings simply to annoy an opponent, or to take utu (satisfaction) for some wrong previously inflicted on them. In this manner court sittings became an extension of – or at least a sequel to – tribal confrontation.

The Native Land Court also became a major institution in Maori life in the late nineteenth and early twentieth centuries. Some old people, repositories of tribal tradition, became almost professional court-goers as claim clashed with counterclaim. More important, perhaps, the court minutes carefully recorded all the evidence and thus became the country's first archive of Maori oral history on a large scale. Families often accompanied elders to sittings in the towns nearest the tribal land under discussion and camped close to the court. Thus the hearings became occasions for reunions and hui.

The national Parliament also instituted four Maori seats, in 1867. One of the factors which made this acceptable to European Members of Parliament was that it gave the North Island a more favourable balance of seats in relation to the South, which had by far the larger population. The early members were kupapa Maori and tended at first to be the nominees and protégés of the Government's Native Minister. They had little contact with the grass roots of Maori communities where national politics (other than the disposal of Maori land) were not at issue. But by the close of the nineteenth century these members were surprising and then annoying successive governments by opposing Maori legislation of the day as not being in the interest of the Maori people. They were not at all effective in changing the course of such legislation in the nineteenth century, but their seats did serve as a Trojan horse to introduce Maori considerations into Parliament and eventually into legislation in the twentieth century, when they were held by more able and more sophisticated members.

By the close of the nineteenth century the prognosis for Maori culture and for the Maori population did not seem favourable. Numbers were falling rapidly, as was the Maori percentage of the population as a whole. From constituting 50 percent of the nation's citizens in 1860, Maori made up only 10 percent by 1891. Their remaining lands constituted only 17 percent of the whole country and a great deal of this was marginal and in effect useless. No money was available for Maori agricultural and pastoral development. While some communities were thriving healthily on their own holdings — most notably those on the East Coast and parts of the Bay of Plenty — others were demoralised and handicapped by malnutrition, alcohol and disease. It was an awareness of these factors in 1907 that led Archdeacon Walsh to write of the 'The Passing of the Maori' in the *Transactions and Proceedings of the New Zealand Institute.* He summarised: 'The Maori has lost heart and abandoned hope. As it has already been observed in the case of the individual, when once the vital force has fallen below a certain point he died from the sheer want of an effort to live; so it is with the race. It is sick unto death, and is already potentially dead.' It was in an attempt to rectify these same conditions that a number of Maori leaders decided to experiment with new forms of political and social activity.

CHAPTER FOUR

RANGATIRATANGA
leadership

At the very time when prospects for Maori survival seemed bleakest, the seeds for racial and cultural recovery were already sown. By the 1890s the population decline had run its course. Maori generally were acquiring immunity from the diseases that had earlier taken such shocking tolls, as a consequence of previous exposure and of marriage with Europeans. Fertility was improving; the birth rate was climbing; and although infant mortality rates remained high, more people were being born and more were surviving. The census of 1901 would show the first documented increase in the Maori population: from 42,000 five years before to 45,000.

Further, political consciousness was fermenting on marae all over the country in the last decade of the nineteenth century. There was talk of claims for land unjustly taken; of seeking redress under the Treaty of Waitangi; of petitioning the Crown to alleviate Maori grievances (two deputations had gone to Britain for this purpose in the 1880s; both were referred back to the New Zealand Government), and of experimenting with new political structures. Inter-tribal hui were being held on a wide scale to debate these and other issues. In the national Parliament a Maori member, James Carroll, was acquiring considerable influence within the ruling Liberal Party. And a group of young Maori, sophisticated in things Maori and Pakeha, were completing their education and laying the foundations for a new style of Maori leadership.

At the same time traditional modes of leadership persisted. In areas where hapu had not been broken up by mortality or alienation of land, hereditary rangatira families still in effect spoke for their communities. Families with ariki claims – Te Heuheus of Ngati Tuwharetoa, Kahui Ariki in Waikato, the Taiaroas in the South Island – still threw up leaders who acted for federations of tribes. But patterns of leadership were changing. Increasingly the way was opening for men, and women, with acquired vocational or organisational skills, quick wits and elo-quence to make bids for community and tribal leadership against or alongside those whose claim was purely hereditary. This was especially so in the case of the small number of Maori pupils who received primary and secondary education, or who trained for a church ministry.

Some among this breed of leaders were prepared to go further than mere lamentation of Maori grievances on Maori marae. They determined to use the system of government to obtain redress and to secure better living and working conditions for their people. In the South Island, such members of the Ngai Tahu tribe used adversity and a sense of injustice to regenerate tribal identity and spirit. Conditions on which they had sold much of their land – that reserves be put aside, hospitals and schools built and landmark boundaries observed – had in many instances been ignored. Ngai Tahu with education and some familiarity with the European world exerted pressure on their rangatira and on tribal runanga to obtain compensation from the Crown for these griev-ances. They formed (or re-formed) committees in South Island kaika, they sent organisers around these settlements (which, being scattered over the whole of the South Island, comprised one of the largest tribal territories in the world), they formed a parliamentary-type body to represent the entire tribe, and they besieged the national Parliament with letters, petitions, deputations and other representations. They elected a succession of Members of Parliament for the specific purpose of promoting their claims – the first instance of widespread Maori agitation resulting in the election of Members of Parliament for a particular purpose.

In Waikato, after failing to persuade the Government to set up a national Maori Parliament, the Maori King Tawhiao set up his own Kauhanganui at Mangakawa near Matamata in 1892. It too debated land claims, especially the question of compensation for the 360,000 Waikato hectares confiscated by the Government in the 1860s. A Kotahitanga or Maori unity movement originating in Northland picked up membership throughout the country, mainly from among traditional rangatira such as Te Heuheu Tukino, and held its own 'Maori Parliament' meetings from 1892 to 1902, latterly at Papawai marae in the Wairarapa under the leadership of Tamahau Mahupuku. All this was novel, in concept and in scale. It looked for a time as though tribalism was being submerged and a feeling resembling Maori nationalism stirring throughout the country. It did not persist, however. The Kingitanga Kauhanganui increasingly became a forum for the Ngati Haua tribe and was deserted by others, including the remainder of Waikato, and the Kotahitanga movement was defused by another which came to be called the Young Maori Party.

The Young Maori Party was not, strictly speaking, a party (some would go further and argue that it was neither young nor, in its origin and orientation, Maori). It was an association of professional men that grew out of the education most of them had received at Te Aute Anglican College in Hawke's Bay. In particular it was a product of the activities of pupils in the 1880s and of Te Aute Old Boys Association in the 1890s. The group was initially known by the cumbersome and pretentious title of the Association for the Amelioration of the Condition of the Maori Race; later it came to be called the Te Aute Association, and later still the Young Maori Party. Its members had come under the commanding influence of the school's headmaster, the Reverend John Thornton, who believed that 'when a weaker nation lives side by side with a stronger one, the weaker, poorer and more ignorant one will die out if it does not emulate the stronger'. This was the ideal he inculcated into his Maori pupils: if the Maori people were to survive they would have to adopt the features of Western nations that had made the latter strong and pre-eminent throughout the world.

The more able and ambitious of Thornton's pupils left Te Aute in the 1880s and 1890s determined to improve the health, literacy and technological progress of the Maori people. They tried to do this at first by holding consciousness-raising meetings among themselves, at which they discussed papers with titles such as 'The decline of the Maori race: its causes and remedies'. These were full of Christian fervour and read like sermons. The pupils themselves have been described as advocating the wholesale adoption of Pakeha culture and the scrapping of surviving elements of their own. 'To them Maori society was degraded, demoralised, irreligious, beset with antiquated, depressing and pernicious customs. Their task... was to reconstruct this society to make the race clean, industrious, sober and virtuous.'

While they were being educated they went out into Maori communities to preach their message of survival through social and religious reform. Some of them devoted school and university vacations to walking tours that took them to rural villages and marae. On one such trip in June 1889, Maui Pomare, Reweti Kohere and Timutimu Tawhai visited a dozen Hawke's Bay settlements over a month, led prayers, and lectured their elders on how to improve their spiritual welfare and material circumstances. All were still pupils at Te Aute.

The most prominent members of the group were Apirana Turupa Ngata of Ngati Porou, Te Rangi Hiroa (Peter Buck) of Taranaki, Maui Pomare of Te Ati Awa, Reweti Kohere and Tutere Wi Repa of Ngati Porou, Edward Pohua Ellison of Ngai Tahu and Frederick Bennett of Te Arawa, although Bennett did not attend Te Aute. Ngata was born in 1874 near Te Araroa on the East Coast of the North Island. He was brought up by an aunt, the wife of the kupapa chief Major Ropata Wahawaha. He was sent to Te Aute at the age of ten and subsequently won a bursary that allowed him to study at Canterbury University College. In 1893 he became the first Maori to obtain a degree when he graduated BA. He then moved to Auckland where he worked for a law firm and studied for an LLB, which he gained in 1897. Committed by this time to a crusade to save the Maori people, Ngata became the full-time travelling secretary for the Young Maori Party. In particular he encouraged and supervised the setting up of Maori tribal committees under the Maori Councils Act of 1900, and he lobbied sympathetic Maori Members of Parliament, especially James Carroll. In 1905 he himself entered Parliament as Member for Eastern Maori, a seat he was to hold for the next 38 years.

The year of Peter Buck's birth is uncertain. It is thought to be 1877. He was the son of an Irish-born settler and a Taranaki Maori mother. Buck spent his early years at his birthplace, Urenui, and attended Te Aute from 1896 to 1898. From there he went on a scholarship to Otago University College and graduated MB and ChB in 1904. He was a Native Health Officer from 1905 to 1909, and in 1909 was elected Member of Parliament for Northern Maori after the death of the former Kotahitanga proponent Hone Heke. The selection and support of a candidate from a tribe outside the electorate was an unprecedented gesture, an act of gratitude to the southern tribes for bringing Heke's body north from Wellington, and an acknowledgement of Buck's outstanding ability.

Buck sat in Cabinet as Minister Representing the Native Race in 1912. In 1914 he contested the Bay of Islands seat unsuccessfully and then enlisted in the Army. After distinguished war service he was appointed Director of Maori Hygiene in 1919. His interests from this time turned increasingly towards ethnology and anthropology, however, and in 1927 he resigned his Health Department post to work for the Bishop Museum in Hawaii. He later became director of the museum and held a chair in anthropology at Yale University. He made only two subsequent visits to New Zealand, and he was knighted in 1946.

Maui Pomare was also from Taranaki, being born north of New Plymouth in 1876 into a rangatira family. He attended Te Aute from 1889 to 1892. In 1893, influenced by a kitchen staff member at the college, he travelled to Michigan in the United States to attend a Seventh-Day Adventist College, from which he graduated MD in 1899, becoming the first Maori doctor. He was appointed a Native Health Officer in 1901, under the Maori Councils Act, and held that position until he entered Parliament as Member for Western Maori in 1911. He served continuously as a Cabinet Minister from 1912 until the Reform Government went out of office in 1928, being responsible successively for the Cook Islands, Health and Internal Affairs. He died in the course of a visit to Los Angeles in 1930.

The initial spearheads for Young Maori Party policies were Buck and Pomare, particularly through their work as Native Health Officers.

Both believed strongly that the Pakeha and Western culture were to be permanent features of New Zealand life, and that the most promising future for the Maori lay in progressive adoption of Western practices, institutions and technology. In particular they advocated health and hygiene measures to halt the population decline, literacy, and the extension of agricultural assistance to Maori land. They also called for a strong degree of individualism in Maori life and the adoption of the Protestant work ethic, and the abolition of what Pomare referred to as the 'pernicious' customs of tohungaism, the tangi and the hui.

Buck wrote in his annual report for 1906: 'The [Maori] communism of the past meant industry, training in arms, good physique, the keeping of the law, the sharing of the tribal burden, and the preservation of life. It was a factor in the evolution of the race. The communism of today means indolence, sloth, decay of racial vigour, the crushing of individual effort, the spreading of introduced infections, diseases, and the many evils that are petrifying the Maori and preventing his advance.' Pomare added: 'The Maori having been an active race and having always been kept in a state of excitement by wars and the rumour of wars, can now only find vent for his feelings on the racecourse, gambling and billiard-playing, with an occasional bout in the Land Court.'

Pomare and Buck also believed that Maori had to introduce individual competition, both amongst themselves and between themselves and Europeans. 'As long as [the Maori] can depend on his communist brother for a meal,' Pomare wrote, 'so long you will have him lazy.' Pomare's and Buck's own careers were to reflect this highly competitive, devil-take-the-hindmost view of life. It contrasted strongly with that of hapu and community cooperation held by traditionally oriented Maori leaders. Both began to feel that they were making insufficient progress in their work as medical officers, however; their clear, well-argued annual reports spoke of the same difficulties year after year. Both felt they were not supported by the Health Department and by Parliament as strongly as they should be, and both concluded they were more likely to bring about policy changes and a commitment of more public funds to Maori health from Parliament itself. Thus they accepted candidacies to join Ngata in the House of Representatives.

The approach of the Young Maori Party to Maori-Pakeha relations, and the approach of its members to Parliamentary tactics, had been pioneered a decade earlier by their mentor James Carroll. Carroll had been born in Wairoa in 1858, son of a Pakeha settler and a Ngati Kahungunu mother. He was sent to primary school in Napier, where he did not show particular aptitude. From the age of twelve he worked on his father's sheep station, then later joined the office of Native Affairs in Wellington, becoming a Native Land Court interpreter. From there he transferred to the job of interpreter in the House of Representatives, which gave him an intimate knowledge of parliamentary procedure and enormous confidence in speaking publicly in both languages.

Carroll first stood for Parliament in 1883, but was defeated for the Eastern Maori seat by Wi Pere. He took the seat in 1887, however, and held it until 1894 when he transferred to the European electorate of Waiapu (later Gisborne). He thus became the first Maori to hold a European parliamentary seat. He was a member of the Liberal Cabinet from 1892 and Minister of Native Affairs from 1897. On several occasions he served as acting-Prime Minister, and he was knighted in 1911.

Carroll believed strongly that the most rewarding strategy for Maori parliamentarians was to compete with Pakeha on their own terms and, where possible, to beat them. This was the advice he gave to Young Maori Party members, especially Ngata, Pomare and Buck. He was popular in Pakeha circles: he never used his Maoriness to reproach his colleagues as some of his predecessors had done. He joined in social occasions with gusto, was a considerable drinker, delivered superb stories and impromptu speeches, and followed horse racing with an impressive knowledge of form and pedigree. His only handicaps in the eyes of his colleagues were a propensity for falling asleep without warning and an alleged reluctance to exert himself.

Carroll frequently subordinated Maori considerations to the policies of the Liberal Party to which he belonged, especially to the party's determination to acquire arable Maori land for European farming and to assimilate the Maori race and culture. He did this because he believed there was no future for Maori separate from that of the Pakeha. When he drew attention to Maori needs it was usually by way of pointing them out as obstacles to be tactically circumvented. Although his tai hoa policy for a time delayed further large-scale acquisition of Maori land, and although he was genuinely sensitive to the difficulties of Maori landowners, he agreed fundamentally with the policies of Prime Minister Seddon and Lands Minister John McKenzie. He believed that the progressive opening up of Maori land for Pakeha leasehold would work to the advantage of Maori owners and Pakeha lessees.

In pursuit of these ends Carroll adopted the role of Maori trouble-shooter for the Liberals. He was frequently sent to hui to contain and mollify Maori opinion; he was used to woo the Maori King Mahuta to accept seats on the Legislative and Executive Councils; he was also often assigned the task of humouring the Maori Members of Parliament. He was rewarded for these things by the trust of his Pakeha colleagues, with the portfolios of Native Affairs and acting-Prime Minister, and with his knighthood, the first given to a Maori. His famous injunction to Maori to hold on to their Maori culture ('kia mau ki to koutou Maoritanga') came late in his career, after World War I, and in his eyes was more a celebration of the role of pageantry in Maori life than a serious proposal for the conservation of Maori values and institutions. The Young Maori Party leaders emerged initially in the Carroll mould, and he was fond of referring to them as his 'young colts'. They admired his commanding presence, his oratory and his capacity for manipulation within the political party system. He encouraged them to follow careers similar to his own. Like him, they had to become national figures at a time when Maori stocks were low in Pakeha eyes and overt racism often rampant. In order to win acceptance for themselves as Maori, they had first to win acceptance as men – and this in effect meant acceptance as Pakeha. Pomare stated this most baldly in 1906: 'There is no alternative but to become a pakeha.' They rejected many features of Maori life that were frowned upon by Europeans; they showed themselves not only as capable as Europeans in competitive situations but often more so. This was the impulse that drove them initially, and the parliamentarians succeeded both in their own and in Pakeha eyes. Young Maori Party views were voiced at Maori meetings around the country from the 1890s, especially by Ngata in his role as travelling secretary. Its members also lobbied Members of Parliament. They convinced Carroll that unless some of the measures demanded by the Kotahitanga movement were adopted, then sitting Maori members would steadily lose support because of the apparent inability of the existing political system to deliver policies that met Maori needs. The major result of this and related submissions on Maori health and welfare was that the Liberal Government passed the Maori Councils Act in 1900. This proposed elected committees to supervise Maori community and tribal affairs with powers comparable to those exercised by Pakeha local authorities.

The tribal committees were expected to supervise sanitation and to suppress those customs that Young Maori Party leaders regarded as pernicious. It was hoped too that they would provide accurate information on births, deaths, marriages and population movements. General conferences were to bring together elected representatives from all over the country, thus doing under official auspices what the Kotahitanga movement had proposed unofficially. In this way the Liberals hoped to diffuse Kotahitanga support; and in this they succeeded. The structure provided by the act itself was not a success, however. The councils were embraced with temporary enthusiasm in some districts and ignored in others. Even in areas where they had met with initial approval they eventually lapsed through a combination of lack of enduring local interest, unfamiliarity with Pakeha committee procedure and lack of commitment to inter-tribal cooperation. By 1910 most councils had ceased to function.

The Tohunga Suppression Act of 1907 was devised by Carroll and Ngata (by then in Parliament) to eradicate what they saw as charlatanism in Maori folk medicine, and to undercut the mana of prophets such as Rua Kenana in the Urewera and Hikapuhi of Te Arawa. Its intention was worthy. The rapid spread of Pakeha-introduced diseases and the profound anxieties they introduced into Maori life had spawned an army of amateur tohunga, untrained in esoteric rites and lore. Maori suffering from illnesses such as influenza, measles and whooping cough sometimes died as a result of immersion in water by 'healers'. But this measure was a more conspicuous failure than the Maori Councils Act. Few prosecutions were brought under it, victims could not or would not give evidence, tohunga practices continued in all Maori districts and the act was eventually repealed in the 1960s.

Some historians and Maori leaders contributed to the view that the programmes and activities of the Young Maori Party were the major factors ensuring the survival of the Maori race and culture. Reweti Kohere, for example, said the party's efforts had 'turned the tide in the history of the Maori People'. That process of survival has even been referred to as a 'Maori Renaissance'. Certainly the Maori population did recover spectacularly from the nineteenth to the twentieth centuries. From the estimated low point of 42,113 in 1896 it rose to 45,549 in 1901, 56,987 in 1921, and increased steadily to more than a quarter of a million by the 1980s. The dying race whose pillow the Victorian liberals had sought to smooth had not merely recovered; it had taken up its bed and walked.

If the claims of the proponents of the Young Maori Party are to be accepted, however, it needs to be shown that the population recovery was a consequence of Young Maori Party activities. And this cannot be established. In his book *The Maori Population of New Zealand 1769–1971*, D. Ian Pool has demonstrated that the Maori birth rate toward the end of the nineteenth century was in fact not low. It was increasing even at a time when the population itself was still decreasing, because fertility was improving. What brought about a steady increase in life expectation from the early 1890s was a decline in the mortality rate. This was based on steady acquisition of immunity to diseases that had previously taken a heavy toll; and to the related reduction in the incidence of epidemics. It is not clear to what extent Pomare's and Buck's sanitation and vaccination programmes from 1900 arrested infection rates, nor what effects the erratic supervisory activities of some Maori councils had on their communities. Pomare reported proudly that by 1908 he had been responsible for the destruction of 1,057 substandard whare and the construction of 1,183 new ones and 839 latrines. As other observers such as Elsdon Best noted, however, the existence of such latrines did not mean that they were used; they were most often abandoned once the medical officer had moved on.

Undoubtedly, Buck and Pomare's activities had some influence on the reduction of the mortality rate, especially in checking the influence of typhoid in some areas. But the more significant causes of the Maori population recovery were an increase in fertility, the decline in epidemics, the related acquisition of immunity through exposure to disease and as a result of marriage with Europeans, and a consequent steady increase in the child-bearing age group. It has to be remembered that Buck and Pomare themselves were often disappointed at the lack of acceptance of their proposals at community level. Indeed, this lack of progress was a reason both cited for entering national politics. The population recovery only became fully apparent after they had become politicians. Their own efforts to assign cause and effect and credit to themselves for the 'renaissance' were largely retrospective exercises in propaganda.

In the field of literacy and education the Young Maori Party leaders made little impact. The models they represented were remote and un-attainable for most Maori of their time. Maori educational achievement beyond primary school remained minimal until after the election of the first Labour Government. Legislation that touched Maori life intimately – that relating to land development, income, social welfare, housing and the settlement of land claims – was not passed until Ngata's pre-eminence from the late 1920s and the formation of the Ratana-Labour alliance from the mid-1930s.

Young Maori Party leaders did not even succeed in communicating with their own people at community level. Buck noted that he was aware of speaking to them as a stranger. Outside their own electorates the Young Maori Party parliamentarians wielded little influence; even within them – with the exception of Ngata – their role was limited. In the two-cosmology view of life that many Maori came to adopt in the twentieth century, parliamentarians were elected to deal with taha Pakeha, the Pakeha aspects of life, not taha Maori. Their experience of frequently being in an adversarial role against community spokesmen from their own electorates (especially in the case of Pomare) and yet not necessarily being rejected by those electorates, was a reflection of this. The subsequent rapid spread of the Ratana Movement in the 1920s and 1930s was a mark of how little the Young Maori leadership and programmes had touched Maori life, and how much the Maori electorates felt their political leaders had still to deliver.

There is a further antidote to the view that Maori affairs in the early twentieth century were dominated by the Young Maori Party. It is the fact that as the incidence of epidemics diminished and families and hapu regained some of their former dimensions and cohesion, Maori community life was far more vigorous than most Pakeha realised. And these communities were in most instances led by immensely able tribal or regional leaders whose qualifications were traditional, local and genealogical. For the most part these men and women were not acknowledged by Pakeha officialdom, nor were they known to Pakeha in general. Unlike the Young Maori Party leaders they did not receive acclamation and knighthoods. But they built up the resources of their communities steadily and regulated the intake of Western elements in a manner that strengthened Maori values and institutions.

They were people such as Eru Ihaka in the far north, Te Puea Herangi in Waikato, Mita Taupopoki of Te Arawa, Numia Kereru of Tuhoe, Te Hurinui Apanui of Ngati Awa, Mihi Kotukutuku of Whanau-a-Apanui, and Teone Taare Tikao of Ngai Tahu on Banks Peninsula. All these and others like them exercised the most effective and most enduring influence over Maori community life up to World War II. They remained solidly and proudly tribal in orientation. They were able to represent their own local interests fairly and to harness community effort. From the 1930s, as a result of Ngata's initiatives in government, some were able to form symbiotic relationships with parliamentarians. There had to be Ngata-type figures in the House of Representatives, to take an overview of what was beneficial and to acquire sufficient expertise and mana to bend the Westminster-based system of legislation and administration towards Maori needs.

Tribalism, however, remained the most potent reality in Maori rural life. To implement his later programmes for cultural and land development, Ngata needed strong allies at hapu and kainga level. Local leaders found that they in turn could strengthen their positions by tapping the resources that Ngata offered, without having to abandon their local power base in a manner that parliamentarians risked. In this way figures like Te Puea, Whina Cooper of Te Rarawa, Hone Heke Rankin of Ngapuhi, Taiporoutu Mitchell of Te Arawa, Rima Whakarua of Taranaki, Hoeroa Marumaru of Rangitikei and Te Kani Te Ua of Ngati Porou were able to increase their influence substantially, successfully supervise local land development and marae building programmes, stimulate community cultural activities and generally raise both standards of living and morale in their own territories. They were not necessarily popular among their own people – in some instances their very lack of popularity was a measure of their bullying success. Some of them, such as Te Puea, Marumaru and Whina Cooper, would eventually become national figures in the process of extending their tribal work into wider fields.

The rise of Te Puea Herangi as a Tainui leader and ultimately a force in national Maori affairs is worthy of special consideration. She was born at Whatiwhatihoe in the King Country in 1883, a grand-daughter of the second Maori King Tawhiao. She achieved prominence within the Kingitanga when she led a campaign against Waikato Maori conscription in World War I. Her claims to leadership as a member of the Kahui Ariki were strengthened greatly by her sharp intellect, quick wits, a high degree of articulateness in Maori and a near-ruthless determination. All these qualities were in evidence when she established Turangawaewae marae at Ngaruawahia from 1921. In the late 1920s the coincidence of her need for further resources with Gordon Coates' and Ngata's plans for Maori cultural and agricultural development brought her into fruitful contact with the governmental and public service network. From this time she was a national Maori figure, Turangawaewae began to take on the character of a national marae, and Te Puea had access to additional resources with which to consolidate her objectives and heighten her mana at home. Ngata's land development scheme was the most dramatic example of this process – it offered a means by which Waikato rural communities could subsist on their own territory and conserve their traditional living patterns. In association with this she developed a calendar of Kingitanga activities in the 1930s and 1940s.

Te Puea used a number of devices to consolidate and extend her programmes. Like other successful local leaders she was an innovator who appealed to precedent. It is difficult to judge the extent to which she chose this or to which the role assumed her. What is apparent is that having decided on a course (moving to Ngaruawahia, building a new meeting house, re-establishing carving and rivercraft, returning to farming) she would always find justification in precedent and tradition, most often in the sayings of her grandfather Tawhiao. Even when breaking with tradition – by standing and speaking in public, for example, which Maori women did not do conventionally – she always made it clear that her own actions should not be taken as reason for discarding tradition. When she devised new programmes – such as raising money by concert tours or inviting political and public service participation in her hui to open Mahinarangi meeting house in 1929 – she cloaked them with traditional Maori activities so as to arouse, quite deliberately, nostalgic memories of past achievements.

While she was succeeding as an innovator appealing to tradition, her innovations themselves became precedents to which she could subsequently appeal to sustain the momentum of her reforms. Hence the Mahinarangi inter-tribal hui presaged and made easier the one to open Turongo House nine years later; and her makeshift hospital shelters and primitive attempts to cope with smallpox and influenza anticipated and helped win acceptance for her fuller health and sanitation programmes in the 1930s and 1940s. She even succeeded in making Western education acceptable as a means of strengthening Maori ties rather than (as conservative Waikato feared) weakening them.

Te Puea's natural aptitudes – in particular her perceptiveness about tactics and the quick-wittedness with which she wrong-footed rivals – were strengthened greatly by her unusual mastery of the arts of organisation and delegation. Her meticulous keeping of records of her activities ensured that she was always well-informed and often better armed than her adversaries. She knew instinctively when to persist in one tactical direction and when to alter course. She was adept at extending her own talents and compensating for skills she lacked by choosing lieutenants to act for her in specialised ways. Her use of Maori and Pakeha mediators made valuable inroads for her in both worlds to an extent she could not have achieved on her own. And at points where people were no longer useful or let her down she was rarely handicapped by sentiment; she simply discarded them.

The immediate consequences of Te Puea's leadership in Waikato can be judged by comparing the legacy she left with the conditions she inherited. She began tribal work in 1910 when Waikato people were largely fragmented and demoralised. In 40 years of relentless effort she found ways for them to return to a system of rural-based extended families, communal patterns of living, the influence of traditional leadership and a calendar of distinctively Maori cultural activities. In addition to these more general goals she was largely responsible for the considerable measure of Pakeha acceptance that the Kingitanga had won by the early 1950s, and she helped mitigate the pain of the land confiscation issue by persuading the Labour Government to pay some compensation to Tainui in 1946. She had also established a model pa and a system of Kingitanga organisation that would eventually survive her. She has been called the most influential woman in New Zealand's political history, and it would be difficult to dispute this assessment.

Some Young Maori Party objectives did eventually come to fruition as a result of Ngata's long tenure of political office. In the 1920s he became a close friend and confidant of the Reform Government Prime Minister Gordon Coates, although they belonged to opposing parties (Ngata remained a Liberal until the party changed its name to United in 1928). Coates was Native Minister from 1921 and Ngata persuaded him to set up the Maori Purposes Fund Board to provide grants for Maori educational, social and cultural activities (the money came from unclaimed interest earned by Native Land Boards). Together they devised the Maori Arts and Crafts Act 1926 to set up a carving school in Rotorua and to encourage Maori art in general. They also collaborated in the establishment of the Board of Ethnological Research to finance the recording and investigation of Maori oral and material culture, and

Ngata himself undertook a study of Maori waiata eventually published in three volumes, and with additional editorial work by Pei Te Hurinui Jones, as *Nga Moteatea*.

Once Ngata replaced Coates as Minister of Native Affairs after the change of government in 1928, the same kinds of measures continued with increased momentum. He made use of large hui — such as that organised by Te Puea for the opening of Mahinarangi meeting house in 1929 — for inter-tribal discussion on broad questions such as how Maori could best share in the kinds of opportunities offered by Pakeha society and on specific topics such as social welfare, land development and the future of Maori language, arts and crafts. In this manner he was able to prepare people for his programmes, gauge reaction, and often shrewdly plant initiatives so that they appeared to come from the people rather than from the Government or the Department of Native Affairs.

The effect of Ngata's cultural policies, allied to his programmes for land development, was a florescence of aspects of Maori culture. There was a sharpening and a strengthening of the arts of Maori oratory on marae throughout the country. Haka and action song were revived for competitive display at the inter-tribal hui. Maori sports meetings intensified competitiveness and strengthened hapu and tribal cohesion. New meeting houses and dining rooms were built in large numbers in the 1930s and 1940s, many of them carved impressively by pupils and graduates of the Rotorua Carving School, such as Pine Taiapa. Grants from the Board of Ethnological Research laid the foundations for Maori social and cultural research, particularly in association with the work of the Polynesian Society, of which Ngata was an enthusiastic member.

In alliance with Ngata and drawing from the resources which he made available, many tribal leaders began cultural revival programmes of their own. Te Puea, for example, established a carving school at Turangawaewae (after her leading carvers had been trained at Rotorua), built a series of meeting houses and other community facilities throughout Waikato and the King Country, revived the construction and ceremonial use of canoes, composed waiata and action songs and trained her TPM concert party for performances throughout the North

Island. The effect of all this, she noted, was 'to make Waikato a people again' – to enhance tribal identity and cohesion.

In the early years of the twentieth century there were reactions against both the elitism of the Young Maori Party and the conservatism of traditional Maori leadership. One was Rua Kenana's Wairua Tapu movement. Rua, a member of the Tamakaimoana hapu of the Tuhoe tribe, was born at Maungapohatu in the Urewera in 1869. His father had died some months earlier fighting alongside Te Kooti Arikirangi. After a series of visions in about 1904, Rua came to believe that he was the brother of Jesus Christ and also the leader that Te Kooti had prophesied would arise to succeed him in the Ringatu Church. As a result of the visions he preached a Maori millennium: everlasting life for Maori who would follow him, and eventual removal of Europeans from New Zealand soil. From 1905 Rua began to carve a 'New Jerusalem' out of the bush at Maungapohatu, one of the most rugged locations for a settlement in the country. Within three years he had attracted over 1,000 Tuhoe, Ngati Awa and Whakatohea followers.

Like other Maori prophets before him, Rua was strongly influenced by the Old Testament, especially by the revelations of God to His chosen people. He identified the Maori people with the Israelites and interpreted scripture accordingly. He also sought complete economic, social and political independence from Pakeha officialdom, believing that the days of the Pakeha occupation of New Zealand were numbered. His community and his preaching were regarded with distaste and suspicion by most Europeans and by Maori leaders such as Carroll and Ngata. An opportunity to exert discouraging pressure on the prophet and his community came in 1911 when he was found to be supplying alcohol to his followers. Between 1911 and 1915 Rua was convicted several times of sly-grogging. When he refused to appear in Court on one of these charges police were sent to arrest him. Rua, misunderstanding the charges and believing he was being persecuted, declined to accompany the police and made provocative remarks about Germans winning the war in which the country was then engaged. A charge of treason was then added to those relating to liquor and resisting arrest.

The climax came in April 1916 when a force of 70 armed police converged on Maungapohatu to arrest the prophet. In the confusion that followed their arrival, shots were exchanged for half an hour, and when they ceased two Maori were dead (including one of Rua's sons), three were wounded, and four policemen injured. The ensuing trial was the longest in New Zealand's legal history to that time. Rua was sentenced to twelve months hard labour and eighteen months reformative treatment. He was released after serving only nine months of these terms.

Rua never recovered completely from the loss of mana which resulted from arrest and imprisonment. His community disintegrated as most of his former followers returned to their previous homes and to the practices of the Ringatu Church (or to the Presbyterian Church, which had begun to evangelise in the Urewera about this time). Rua himself continued to lead a smaller group of Iharaia (Israelites) until his death at Matahi in 1937. The movement had been a further example of an attempt to find a Maori path to the Judaic-Christian God that excluded the Western trappings of European Christianity. It also represented an attempt to establish rangatiratanga or separate Maori authority in New Zealand.

The movement founded by Tahupotiki Wiremu Ratana had different roots from those of the Young Maori Party and Rua's Wairua Tapu religion. It was neither elitist nor traditionalist in origin, although it did draw on Maori precedents for prophetic movements. It arose from the leadership vacuum that developed in some Maori communities in the early years of the twentieth century. On the one hand there were the Young Maori Party 'modernisers', working at parliamentary and public service level to try to improve the lot of Maori nationally. At community level there were the local leaders operating according to traditional conditions and conventions. Increasingly, however, there was a group of Maori who were not touched by either of these brands of leadership: people who lived in communities in which traditional leadership structures had fallen into disuse, or people who had moved to communities outside their own tribal territory. Many such Maori were utterly unmoved by and uncomprehending of the kind of directions offered by the Young Maori Party. They were leaderless and yet seeking leadership, but of a kind that was Maori rather than tribal, and populist rather than elitist. And they found it in T.W. Ratana.

Ratana was a ploughman from the Rangitikei district south of Wanganui. He began his spiritual mission in November 1918 when he was 45 years old. He said subsequently that he was sitting on the verandah of his family home looking out to sea when a small cloud arose from the water and hovered over the house. From it Ratana heard the voice of God telling him that He had selected the Maori to be His chosen people, and that Ratana's mission was to unite them and turn them to God. In the wake of this experience Ratana prepared himself for this role. He read the Bible closely, and a book called *Health for the Maori* by J.H. Pope (which had been one of the texts most valued by members of the Young Maori Party). Then he began to preach the kotahitanga or essential unity of the Maori people and to practise faith healing, initially among his own family and then among a wider congregation. People began to visit him from all over the country as his reputation spread.

Unlike other Maori leaders of the time Ratana was not of rangatira status and did not have a recognisable hapu or tribal base; nor was he well educated in the Western sense; nor, even, especially charismatic. He was a man of ordinary appearance and mannerism driven by an extraordinary mission. Much of his success can be understood in the light of the social climate in which he preached, and from the fact that the Maori people at large were then reeling from the physical and psychological effects of the influenza epidemic, which took five times as many Maori lives as non-Maori. Further, many Maori servicemen had returned from World War I impatient with the conservatism, the inertia and the technological backwardness of rural Maori communities. They sought leadership that offered material progress for Maori.

Ratana provided leadership that met these diverse needs. From his reading of the Bible he offered an Old Testament explanation for the displacement and suffering of the Maori people as God's chosen race, and he promised deliverance from these tribulations. Although he was emphatically Maori in his use of language and metaphor, he rejected many traditional practices and values such as tribalism, tangihanga, tapu, tohungaism and carving. His faith-healing successes were so spectacular that a settlement grew around his house and came to be called Ratana Pa. The museum there took on the appearance of a New Zealand Lourdes as it filled with discarded crutches, wheelchairs and spectacles. Ratana, now called the Mangai (mouthpiece of God) by his followers, began to travel and carry his preaching and healing to all parts of the country. He had a special appeal to those he called the Morehu – the growing number of detribalised, non-chiefly common people, most of them subsistence farmers, farm labourers or rural town workers.

From 1922 the Ratana Movement that had formed around the Mangai became preoccupied increasingly with politics. It campaigned for statutory ratification of the Treaty of Waitangi as a panacea for Maori difficulties, and it circulated a petition (which eventually collected over 30,000 signatures) calling for this measure. When the Mangai's oldest son Tokouru contested Western Maori in the 1922 General Election, he astonished political observers by coming to within 800 votes (3,037 to 3,835) of unseating the experienced Maui Pomare. Clearly the face of Maori affairs was changing; Ratana and his followers constituted a political force as well as a spiritual one. In 1928 Ratana declared the end of his spiritual mission and the beginning of his temporal one. He vowed to place his chosen representatives – the Four Quarters – into all four Maori parliamentary seats.

Support for the movement fell away nationally in the 1928 and 1931 General Elections. But in 1932 Eruera Tirikatene took Southern Maori in a by-election. With the intensification of the Great Depression the Ratana bandwagon gathered momentum. Candidates made much of the fact that unemployment benefits for Maori were lower than those for Europeans and far more difficult to obtain. They continued to use the Treaty of Waitangi as a symbol for Pakeha breaches of faith with Maori. And they adopted American-style campaign techniques in the form of brass bands, rosettes and rallies.

The movement struck an informal alliance with the New Zealand Labour Party for the 1931 election. Ratana candidates, although nominally independent, would vote with Labour if elected; Labour in turn would not put up official candidates against them. When Tirikatene took his seat in Parliament the following year he was escorted by the Labour whips. In the 1935 election he was joined by Tokouru Ratana in Western Maori. Labour, in becoming the Government with a landslide majority, increased its appeal in the eyes of the Ratana Movement. The Mangai visited the new Prime Minister Michael Joseph Savage and formalised the association between the two movements in a manner that was characteristic:

'Ratana... placed on the table before him four objects: a potato, a broken gold watch, a greenstone tiki and a huia feather. The Mangai explained their meaning. The potato was the ordinary Maori, needing his land. The watch was the law relating to the lands of the Maori. Only the machinery of the law could repair the law. The greenstone tiki stood for the traditions and mana of the Maori. And the huia feather, the sign of a paramount chief, would be worn by Mr Savage if he would look after his Maori people. The Prime Minister accepted the proposal.'

Ratana electoral support gathered further momentum from this time. Paraire Paikea took Northern Maori in 1938. And in 1943 Tiaki Omana did what most observers believed was impossible: he toppled Ngata in Eastern Maori. The Ratana hegemony was now complete: the Four Quarters held the four Maori seats; the prophecy of the Mangai was fulfilled. And Labour was able to count on retaining those seats for the next 30 years. The alliance between the two movements was cemented by the policies of the Labour Government and by the continuing success of Ratana candidates at the polls, partly as a consequence of those policies.

Labour legislation introduced the secret ballot for Maori electors, equalised unemployment benefits and opportunities for housing finance, raised expenditure on Maori health and education, provided social security and the first Maori welfare officers, and addressed contentious land claims in the South Island and Waikato. These latter negotiations did much to consolidate support for Labour in the areas that benefited. It was not simply a matter of monetary gain; it was also a public acknowledgement that many of the Maori grievances from the nineteenth century had been justified. In addition, Maori workers shared in the resumption and expansion of post-Depression economic activity – more spectacularly than Pakeha in many instances because their previous plight had been more acute.

The result of these measures was that although Ratana Members of Parliament were less conspicuously able than some of their predecessors and their political opponents, they were nonetheless able to point to a body of legislation that had improved the material circumstances of the Maori people dramatically. As one Maori writer has noted, 'it was inevitable that Ratana MPs should present these developments as... a delivery of their election promises... Because these benefits persisted, the Ratana claim to have substantially lifted the Maori standard of living has been self-perpetuating and self-justifying.'

CHAPTER FIVE

TaHa Maori, TaHa PakeHa

two peoples

For the first half of the twentieth century the Maori population remained located largely where it had been in the late nineteenth century (see page 51). This meant that in effect there were two New Zealands, one Maori and one Pakeha. They were insulated from one another geographically, socially and culturally. As a consequence race relations were initially a far less dominant feature of New Zealand life in the first half of the twentieth century than they had been in the nineteenth: they were a less noticeable aspect of day-to-day life and they did not require (or receive) anything like the same degree of attention from the architects of government policy.

The reasons for this are not difficult to understand. In addition to the location of Maori population there was its size and its relationship to the population of the country as a whole. In 1850 there had been some 50,000 Maori in a total population of less than 100,000. By 1857 Maori still represented 48.6 percent of the total. At the same time a large number were armed and in effective control of large sections of the central North Island. By 1901 the Maori population had dropped to about 45,000 and represented only 5.6 percent of the total – a percentage drop of more than 40 in 50 years. Even with the subsequent recovery in Maori numbers the proportion did not rise to more than 8 percent. By the turn of the twentieth century, therefore, there were fewer Maori than there had been previously; and they were to remain a far smaller percentage of the total population than they had been at mid-nineteenth century.

Further, Maori who had survived were not considered the threat — whether visible or latent — to European settlement and civilisation that some of their parents and grandparents had seemed to represent. By 1900 they were no longer armed on a large scale. And, although they were largely in settlements remote from centres of Pakeha population, the Queen's law was established unequivocally throughout the country. At the slightest suggestion of Maori intransigence — at Waima in 1898 or at Maungapohatu in 1916, for example — the authorities moved swiftly to meet threatened force with greater force and to deter other would-be aggressors. When Rua Kenana was eventually tried on charges relating to seditious language and sly-grogging, the judge presiding made it clear that the real issue at stake was one of authority:

'You have learned that the law has a long arm, that it can reach you, however far back into the recesses of the forest you may travel, and that in every corner of the great Empire to which we belong the King's law can reach anyone who offends against him. That is the lesson that your people should learn from this trial.' ('Your people' and similar judicial references at this time seemed to suggest that when Pakeha were on trial it was as individuals; when Maori were before the courts it was as representatives of their race. This too illustrated a gap between the two peoples.)

There had also been a degree of Maori withdrawal from contact with Europeans. In 1900 the bulk of the Maori population of 45,000 lived in scattered rural communities that were Maori in composition and orientation. Some who had formerly seen a good deal of Pakeha and traded with them extensively — such as Waikato and Bay of Plenty tribes — were seeing far less of them by 1900 in the still-bitter wake of defeat in war and land confiscations. The tendency throughout the country was for Maori to get on with their lives in their own territories; and for non-Maori to get on with theirs in other territories.

The general view of Pakeha officialdom in national and in local body administration was that it was better for Maori to be living in rural districts than in towns; and that this location gave them an opportunity to live off the land and not be a drain on the public purse, and to practise aspects of their lifestyle (hui, tangi, Maori values) that Europeans found distasteful.

In fact, the rural distribution of the Maori population was not necessarily advantageous for Maori themselves. The Maori work force in the early twentieth century could best be described as a rural proletariat, part of it land-owning but not land-using; part of it disinherited by alienation of land. Only on the East Coast of the North Island and in northern Hawke's Bay was Maori farming carried on in an organised and sustained manner. And these operations had come about in part because sympathetic Pakeha such as the Williams family had been prepared to help finance such operations in the absence of government assistance. Few Maori individuals at this time could be described as wealthy in European terms. Those who could have been – rangatira families who held title to large tracts of land or who had leased or sold such land – had strong community and tribal demands made upon their monetary and other material resources. Aroha and mana gave status to distribution, not to accumulation.

Maori individuals and communities without land had lost it as a consequence of confiscation (Waikato, Bay of Plenty and Taranaki tribes); as a consequence of what was later deemed to be unfair purchase (the Ngai Tahu and Ngati Mamoe tribes of the South Island and the Muriwhenua of the far north); or by the orthodox temptations of lease and sale. Even where they had inherited land interests, however, these were frequently uneconomic because that land was often marginal (which was why Pakeha purchasers had overlooked it in the first place); because it could not be brought into production without heavy capital investment; or because of the administrative divisions brought about by multiple ownership. Sometimes all three handicaps applied. And Maori farmers, unlike Pakeha farmers, were not eligible for assistance from public funds.

Maori, then, were geographically, socially and administratively segregated from contact with Pakeha, and – in the case of non-rangatira who could not attend inter-tribal hui – from contact with Maori from other districts and tribes. There was no social and cultural interaction between Maori and Pakeha on a wide scale. Such contact as there was, was limited largely to land dealings, rural employment, and to the minimal effort of governmental authorities to implement policies on Maori health and education. The latter involved only a small number of Europeans and very little expenditure of public money.

With few exceptions, Europeans in New Zealand did not want to draw from the cultural and emotional reserves of Maori life. The only asset Maori held that interested most non-Maori was land. And it was the continuing need to acquire Maori land by sale or lease for an expanding Pakeha population and agricultural economy that shaped most governmental policies towards Maori. Maori for their part were forced to accept what they had not appreciated in 1850: that the European colonisation of New Zealand was permanent and irreversible. For many of them this was a source of trauma and depression, an additional reason to withhold themselves from non-Maori aspects of New Zealand life.

One way of charting the gulf between the two peoples* is to survey the writing by Europeans about Maori from the turn of the century. Such literature tended to be either hostile or patronising. Expressions of hostility in newspaper articles and (especially) letters to the editor were often undisguisedly racist and employed terms such as 'blacks' and 'niggers', and favoured such adjectives to describe Maori as 'dirty', 'degraded', 'lazy' and 'immoral'. Articles and cartoons were sometimes almost xenophobic in their views of the Maori being Maori – as if such people had no right to live in a country colonised by Europeans. (Similar feelings were directed against other non-Anglo-Saxons such as Jews, Chinese and Dalmatians.) Coon humour, which portrayed Maori as simpletons who were comic in their inability to cope with Western civilisation, was common on postcards, in newspaper cartoons and in photographic journals such as the *Auckland Weekly News*.

---

* It could be argued, of course, that Pakeha New Zealanders with their varied backgrounds did not constitute 'one people' at this time. For the most part, however, they were British; and they submerged minor differences in class, occupation and ethnic traditions to participate in a British political, legal and administrative system with a facility and willingness that Maori could not match.

The patronising writers were at least motivated for the most part by humanitarianism and compassion. Many of them had a *fin de siécle* interest in characters described in terms such as 'the last of the old type of better Maori'. The leading practitioner of this perception and style was historian and journalist James Cowan, who felt considerable regret about the extent to which Western intrusion in New Zealand had fragmented Maori culture.

According to this view, there had been much about the pre-European Maori that was noble and dignified. There had been old-world courtesies, codes of honour, psychic and spiritual perceptions, handsomeness and virility in 'pure-bred' chieftains and warriors, and dusky beauty in maidens of similar pedigree. According also to this view, contact with Western things had tainted these qualities and manners. Throughout the nineteenth century Maori had been in physical, cultural and moral decline as a consequence of abandoning old ways and of prolonged contact with alcohol and disease. Cowan tended to view his elderly informants as survivors from a pristine age, as men and women who exemplified the most worthy features of their culture, which were destined for extinction. One of them, Hauauru of Araikotore near Kihikihi, he described in this manner:

'[He] is a picturesque figure who, in my memories of the past, personifies much of the departed savage glory of the Maori race. He typified the splendid dying manhood of his people. Born in the New Zealander's Stone Age, he survived to near the end of the miracle-working white man's nineteenth century, flotsam of the primitive world stranded on the shores of modern progress... A Homeric personality was that of this old cannibal warrior, a savage but a gentleman, full of courteous friendly feeling for the whites whom he had once fought and bitterly hated, and full of the hospitable generosity of the true Maori *rangatira...*'

Such a view was limiting on several counts. First, it sentimentalised Maori life to the point of unreality. At whatever point writers chose to 'freeze' history there would always have been Maori whom they regarded as 'good' and 'bad', courteous and discourteous, traditionalists and innovators, activists and idlers. Secondly, it suggested that everything worthwhile about Maori life lay in the past and would soon be lost irretrievably. And thirdly it tended to blind observers to many of the fascinating and innovative phases of adaption that Maori were experiencing in local communities in the early years of the twentieth century.

Again reflecting the conventions of his time, Cowan invested his Maori work with a mystique that was not present when he was writing about the same period of non-Maori history and experience. His information, he noted, had been gathered 'around the camp fire on summer nights on the shores of one or other of the beautiful lakes in the Rotorua country, in the Taranaki bush, in the settlements of the King Country and Taupo, in the houses of the Waikato canoe-men, in the bark-roofed *wharepunis* of the Urewera.' The italicisation of Maori words, a convention for the use of 'foreign' concepts and words, exemplified the extent to which Maori things were then viewed by Europeans as exotic in the land of their origin.

All this was undeniably well-intentioned. It did at least place some value on Maori perceptions and customs. It suggested Maori displayed worthy qualities abandoned by rationalist, acquisitive and individualistic Western communities. And it suggested this at a time when racism was rife in some pockets of New Zealand life. Yet Cowan's views, with their gauze of romanticism, also served to place Maori and Maori considerations into a kind of never-never land, safely beyond the political and social preoccupations of contemporary New Zealand life. According to such a vision Maori would not be seen as claimants on the national purse and conscience, their social and economic difficulties would not be viewed as the responsibilities of the country as a whole. They receded to being merely a colourful element from New Zealand's past, surviving in the mountainous and rural hinterlands.

The imaginative equivalent of Cowan's writing was the fiction of authors such as Alfred Grace, William Satchell and F.O.V. Acheson. They depicted romantic Maori figures – noble heroes, beautiful and tragic heroines, unrequited love – through a haze of poetic imagery. These figures bore little relation to life and conditions in twentieth-century Maori communities; and for the most part they made no

distinctions between Maori of different regions, tribes and hapu –
distinctions that would have been crucial in Maori eyes and in fact.

From the 1930s more able writers (Frank Sargeson, Roderick
Finlayson, Maurice Shadbolt and others) devised far more credible
Maori characters and situations, and ones that were closer to the
realities of Maori life. There were still elements of unconscious
patronisation, however, 'the temptation... to find in the Maori virtues
that are missing in the Pakeha and to use him as a criticism of Pakeha
society'. There was also a continuation of stereotyping ('happy-go-
lucky, lazy people, mostly not too bright... or the big-brown-eyes and
little-bare-feet touch'), and severe difficulties in conveying Maori
English. Fiction involving Maori did not lose these elements of awk-
wardness nor reflect the variegated patterns of Maori experience until
imaginative writers who were also Maori, most notably Witi Ihimaera,
Patricia Grace and Keri Hulme, emerged in the 1970s.

In non-fiction, apart from the able ethnologists such as Elsdon Best
and Peter Buck (both of whom, like Cowan, tended to equate Maori
adaptation to Western influences with pollution of a formerly pure
stream of culture), the earliest perceptive writers on Maori matters were
the journalist Eric Ramsden, who made earnest and frequently successful attempts from the 1920s to interpret Maori preoccupations to
non-Maori audiences and to Pakeha in authority; and I.L.G. Sutherland,
New Zealand's first recognised social scientist. Sutherland and his
successors Ernest Beaglehole and James Ritchie highlighted reasons for
lack of Maori advancement in socio-economic terms as well as in
cultural ones. With Ramsden, they deserve much of the credit for public
discussion and policies in the 1940s and 1950s that were related towards
Maori needs, while at the same time recognising the intrinsic worth of
Maori ritual and values. Such discussion eventually gave weight to the
concept of New Zealand as a bi-cultural rather than a purely Anglo-
Saxon society.

There was no comparable body of literature to mirror Maori views
of Pakeha over the same period. But what has been published by way
of reminiscence by writers such as Amiria Stirling and Reweti Kohere
suggests that there was a Maori stereotype of the Pakeha as someone

who was self-centred, materialist, acquisitive, unfeeling about their extended family and callous about their treatment of the dead. By highlighting and caricaturing European qualities that were distasteful in Maori eyes, Maori commentators such as Te Puea Herangi also communicated indirectly the qualities they valued most according to their own mores. And these too suggested a wide and continuing cultural gap between most Maori and most Pakeha.

Throughout the first half of the twentieth century there were a few aspects of wider New Zealand life in which Maori sought to participate, and in which they were accepted by the Pakeha majority. The most notable (and noticeable) was warfare. Traditional Maori communities had, for the most part, placed high value on prowess in battle. This valuation persisted through the periods of the musket and the New Zealand Wars. After the 30-odd years of peace that followed the Te Kooti campaign, some Maori actively sought opportunities to keep the warrior tradition alive. James Carroll believed it could be a factor that would restore vigour to languishing Maori communities. He himself had fought in the Te Kooti skirmishes and he was keen to lead a force of 300 Maori to put down an apparent uprising in difficult terrain in Samoa in 1899. After the outbreak of the South African War that same year a large meeting at the Basin Reserve in Wellington, dominated by Tamahau Mahupuku, called on the Government to dispatch a Native Contingent to the war. Neither of these proposals was accepted. Up to 1914 the Imperial Government in London refused to allow the use of coloured colonials alongside or against white troops. A number of Maori with European names succeeded in enlisting for the South African War in the New Zealand contingents, however, and they served with distinction.

With the outbreak of World War I fifteen years later, the Imperial Government at first allowed recruitment of Maori for garrison duties and then, with the Gallipoli campaign, for combat. To Maori Members of Parliament, and to Pomare in particular, it was essential that Maori show themselves to be the equals of Pakeha in recruitment and casualty rates. Only this, they believed, would prove that Maori were worthy of equal consideration in civilian life. The members formed a recruitment committee and stumped the country to raise volunteers for what eventually became the Pioneer Battalion. Peter Buck sailed with the first contingent to Egypt. Once casualties began to occur in Gallipoli and later in France, the committee redoubled its efforts to enlist reinforcements to obtain utu and to sustain the battalion's strength.

The campaign was not an unqualified success, however. Although some 2,200 Maori men volunteered for service (about 20 percent of the eligible group) and almost half this number became casualties, the committee found it extremely difficult to maintain the promised reinforcement quotas. Some tribes – Te Arawa, Ngati Porou, Ngai Tahu – contributed disproportionately (they tended to be the kupapa ones). Others, such as Taranaki with a confiscation grievance, gave scarcely any men. Later drafts had to be swollen by Rarotongans and Niue Islanders, and even they did not come up to strength. The Waikato in Pomare's own electorate refused to enlist at all and were conscripted towards the end of the war as a punishment (conscription was not applied to Maori in general).

The overall Maori contribution to the war effort, however, especially the combat record, had the effect sought by the Maori Members of Parliament. It showed the Maori to be, Pomare suggested, 'the peer of any man on earth', and it made it more difficult for the country's Pakeha leaders to argue in favour of excluding Maori from full participation in national life. It also raised hopes among ex-Battalion members that conditions of wartime equality with Pakeha soldiers would continue into peacetime. They did not. Legislation forbidding Maori to buy alcohol and excluding them from housing and farm development finance persisted after the war. Few Maori soldiers were eligible for rehabilitation assistance. These conditions were among those that drove many ex-servicemen into the ranks of the Ratana Movement.

The Maori response to World War II was even more wholehearted and showed the extent to which the race had become more integrated into the national life in the intervening 25 years. Without conscription (which was again applied to Pakeha only) and with no organised opposition to recruitment, over 17,000 Maori enlisted for combat and

11,500 took places in essential industries, many of the latter moving from rural districts into towns to do so. The Maori Battalion covered itself in glory as a combat unit in North Africa and Italy, and individual soldiers such as Victoria Cross winner Moananui-a-Kiwa Ngarimu and battalion commander Arapeta Awatere were regarded as heroes by all New Zealand troops.

At home the Maori contribution to the war was coordinated by the Maori War Effort Organisation, which was designed specifically to overcome some of the difficulties experienced in the previous war (remembered by Ngata, who was still in Parliament). It was officially recognised by the Government and the Member for Northern Maori, Paraire Paikea, was co-opted into Cabinet as Minister in Charge of the Maori War Effort. Under Paikea's direction and with the support of the other Maori members, the organisation appointed recruiting and liaison officers at tribal level. It also set up 407 tribal committees and 60 executives to encourage enlistment, to mobilise men and women for work in essential industries, to direct the growing of crops specifically needed for the war effort, to raise funds for the Red Cross and to collect comfort items for Maori prisoners of war and troops at the front.

The effect of both battalion service and the success of the Maori War Effort Organisation was to increase Maori consciousness over tribal feeling, and to enlarge Maori confidence. Maori as a recognisably separate ethnic group with distinctive ways of organising themselves had contributed inter-tribally to a successful national effort. Again servicemen returned home expecting and this time demanding equality of treatment with their Pakeha compatriots, and this time they were far more successful in achieving it. Maori land development schemes were expanded significantly as a rehabilitation measure, and Maori were also eligible for business loans, tools-of-trade loans, trade training and other educational assistance.

Throughout the period Maori also attended Agricultural and Pastoral shows in districts where they lived in proximity to Pakeha farmers. They were especially keen to engage in sport amongst themselves, and against Pakeha individuals and teams. A and P show competitions (athletics, wood-chopping, tug-of-war) were among the most popular;

there were also horse racing, cycling, hockey, tennis, golf, basketball and river regattas.

But apart from warfare, the one national activity to which Maori contributed in a measure resembling their full potential was rugby football. The first Maori to represent New Zealand overseas went on a tour of Britain and Australia in 1888–89 as the 'New Zealand Native Team'. Other tours followed from 1910. Within New Zealand there were Maori clubs, internal Maori tours, a Maori Advisory Board of the New Zealand Rugby Football Union from 1922, and from 1928 the country was divided into four Maori districts to compete annually for a trophy provided by the Prince of Wales.

Maori were also welcomed into the country's national representative team, the All Blacks. Those who distinguished themselves – George Nepia, Lui Paewai, Ben Couch, Pat Walsh, Waka Nathan, Sid Going – acquired the status of national heroes during their playing days. In this sphere at least there was no reluctance to recognise or accept Maori talent, except in the case of tours of that other great rugby-playing nation, South Africa. On such occasions Maori players were stood down, the first time being from a New Zealand Army Team in 1919. This created some ill-feeling throughout the country although not, apparently, among the Maori players themselves. The differences between New Zealand and South Africa were highlighted in 1921, however, when a Maori team played the Springboks at Napier. A South African journalist filed a report for his own paper that was intercepted and published by the local *Daily Telegraph*:

'... it was bad enough having to play a team officially designated New Zealand natives, but the spectacle of thousands of Europeans frantically cheering on a band of coloured men to defeat members of their own race was too much for the Springboks, who were frankly disgusted.'

When protests against such attitudes and against the participation of New Zealand players in a racially segregated system within South Africa were finally made, they came from the wider New Zealand community, not from rugby players or the New Zealand Rugby Union. Until 1960, however, the vast majority of New Zealanders continued to tolerate South African dictation of the racial composition of All Black teams to tour that country.

Participation in rugby within New Zealand did much to enhance a positive sense of Maoriness in Maori communities; and it offered one of the few occasions on which Pakeha could view a Maori activity that they understood and approved of wholeheartedly. The only other occasions on which Maori were 'on display' to citizens who would not otherwise encounter them as a group were Royal Tours, and National Exhibitions such as those held in Christchurch in 1906, in Dunedin in 1925 and in Wellington for the centennial of British sovereignty in 1940.

The Royal Tours were those of the Duke and Duchess of Cornwall in 1901, the Prince of Wales in 1920, the Duke and Duchess of York in 1927 and the Duke of Gloucester in 1935. For all these visits Maori were assembled at Rotorua for a single national welcome and display of loyalty and Maori culture. Most tribes went along with this arrangement, albeit with reservations. Many were scornful of the extent to which the Arawa hosts had oriented their Maori activities around the entertainment of tourists; some, such as successive leaders of the Kingitanga, boycotted the function on the grounds that they wanted to welcome Royal visitors on their own territory, as Pakeha New Zealanders were able to do. Tour organisers believed that one Maori welcome was as much as Royal Personages could endure, and they were worried about the risks of food poisoning. Disagreements over such matters were always between Maori and Pakeha officialdom, never with royalty. Maori loyalty to the British Crown and its representatives was a constant feature of Maori-Pakeha relations up to the 1980s.

The National Exhibitions also highlighted Maori culture but – concentrating as they did on carving, costume and action songs – they did so in a manner that was nostalgic and decorative. They may have helped win acceptance of Maori material as pleasingly exotic elements from New Zealand's past. But, like the displays for tourists at Rotorua and the haka and action song performances of itinerant concert parties, they gave non-Maori little indication of the nature and day-to-day strengths of Maori values for those who were committed to them.

The preoccupations of government policies relating to Maori remained land, health and education, and by far the greatest of these was land. Between 1892 and 1911 the Liberal Government purchased a total of 1.2 million hectares of Maori land, leaving about 2.8 million hectares in Maori ownership. The Reform Government which came to office in 1912 was farmer-dominated and its two Native Affairs Ministers were also farmers: William Herries and Gordon Coates. Not surprisingly it too sought to continue the acquisition of Maori land and did so with the support of its sole Maori Member, Maui Pomare.

Between 1912 and 1920 Maori holdings were further reduced from 2.8 million to 1.8 million hectares, and of that 1.8 million 310,800 were unsuitable for development and 300,000 were already leased to Pakeha farmers.

Throughout this period, as a member of the Opposition, Apirana Ngata worked virtually on his own to explore organisational and legislative measures that could surmount the difficulties of Maori land development and administration. With his own Ngati Porou people he evolved management of land by incorporated committees (of which the Mangatu Incorporation was later the most successful), and a system of consolidation that allowed exchanges of interests to group land blocks into economic holdings. These experiments were limited largely to the East Coast and the Urewera until the mid-1920s, when other tribes began to adopt them with the encouragement of the Native Land Court. By that time Ngati Porou owned nearly a quarter of a million sheep and had their own dairy company, a finance company and a cooperative store.

When Ngata became Native Affairs Minister in 1928 he was able to devise legislation to assist Maori farmers on a national basis for the first time. His Native Land Amendment and Native Claims Adjustment Act allowed the advance of public money for clearing and development work on Maori farms – up to three-fifths of the value of the property, allocated through local land boards. These loans were repaid from subsequent agricultural production. The schemes were operated largely by Maori labour under Maori leadership, and Ngata was assiduous about recruiting the talents and mana of energetic local leaders such as Te Puea Herangi and Taiporoutu Mitchell.

In 1934, Ngata's administration of his portfolio was investigated by a Royal Commission. This found him guilty of disregarding accepted channels of communication, of not adequately accounting for the expenditure of State funds, and of using State funds in the interest of his own family and tribe. None of these were criminal matters. But, unsupported by his colleagues and under fierce attack from the Labour Opposition, Ngata resigned from Cabinet. He never regained ministerial office. The land schemes themselves were regarded as being sufficiently successful to be carried on by subsequent administrations, however.

Throughout the period of Ngata's ministry New Zealand moved steadily into the grip of the worldwide Depression. Maori rural workers began to suffer as Pakeha farmers and local bodies laid off their contract workers. In rural towns the small number of Maori salaried employees were the first to be displaced by staff reductions. There was a feeling in Government and among the public at large that, unlike Pakeha, Maori could simply 'go home to the pa' for food and shelter. By 1933 they made up an estimated 40 percent of the total unemployed and they were paid lower benefits than non-Maori.

The situation was relieved after the election of the Labour Government in 1935. One of its first measures was to abolish the unequal benefit rates; and the expansion of economic activity in the late 1930s brought a degree of temporary prosperity to many of the land development schemes and created additional employment in rural areas. Social Security greatly increased the spending power of extended families with its provision of additional income for children and for the aged. Labour modified earlier requirements that had made it difficult and frequently impossible for Maori without adequate documentation of birth to secure child allowances and old-age pensions. A study in one district noted that, 'From the Maori [Social Security] has removed some of the fear of grinding poverty which has been... the major anxiety of their lives.'

Reports on health and sanitation in most areas of Maori population remained critical of conditions until well into the 1930s. This was an embarrassing blot on the record of a nation that claimed racial equality.

The one major element of progress was that the incidence of the kinds of epidemics that had mown down the Maori population in the nineteenth century was kept low. The last major one was the Influenza Epidemic (the 'Great Flu') of 1918 in which at least 1,130 Maori died, a rate 4.5 times greater than that for Europeans. The actual death rate for Maori was higher, because figures were not collected in many communities. Peter Buck called it 'the severest setback the race has suffered since the days of Hongi Hika.'

In the 1930s tuberculosis, typhoid fever, dysentery, diarrhoeal and respiratory diseases persisted and were taking a disproportionate toll on Maori life. In 1938 the Maori death rate per 1,000 people was 24.31; that for non-Maori 9.71. The Maori infant mortality rate was 153.26 per 1,000 live births as against 36.63 for others. No real progress was made in reducing these figures until the Labour Government drastically improved Maori housing in the 1930s and 1940s; and until Maori health was made the responsibility of the Health Department's district medical officers. This last measure succeeded because it presented 'a direct challenge to bring the state of Maori health to a standard more comparable with that of Europeans, and medical officers could no longer look to anyone else as being responsible for doing this.'

The individual most responsible for lifting standards of Maori health was Dr H.B. Turbott, first as South Auckland Medical Officer and later as Director of School Hygiene. He lobbied the Labour Minister of Health (and later Prime Minister) Peter Fraser for special appropriations for Maori health projects. Turbott's most efficacious programmes were persuading the Government to provide tanks and privies for Maori homes, installed by local labour; and persuading Maori on a wide scale to seek treatment for tuberculosis and to agree to a degree of isolation for this treatment, often in well-ventilated portable huts provided by the Health Department. Turbott also directed District Health Nurses towards preventative work, especially with children, and he developed good working relations with local leaders such as Te Puea.

The combination of all these measures along with the general lifting of Maori incomes in the post-Depression years brought spectacular improvements in Maori health over two decades. The death rate from tuberculosis dropped from an estimated 50 per 10,000 of population in 1933 to 10.06 in the early 1950s, and 3.82 in 1956–60. The incidence of typhoid dropped right down. Infant mortality rates fell, though less dramatically. And the general life expectancy for Maori rose from 46.6 years for males and 44.7 for females in 1925–27 to 57 and 59 in 1956–57.

Apart from geographical isolation, one reason Maori remained conspicuously absent from most areas of national life in the first half of the twentieth century was that the numbers receiving secondary and tertiary educational qualifications were low. Hence Maori were poorly represented in the professions and in business. This was caused in part by rural-urban segregation of the races, which meant that Maori families often lived considerable distances from State secondary schools; in part by cultural and sociological factors which discouraged Maori parents from placing a high value on educational qualifications; and in part by the policies pursued by successive governments.

Up to the 1930s Maori education in both denominational and State-run schools reflected the ideology that had led to official acceptance of Ngata's land schemes in 1929: that the future life of Maori was to be worked out in rural areas. This view was reflected in 1931 in a major policy statement by the Director of Education: '... the best means for [Maori] to realise the full benefits of civilisation is through the cultivation of land... These considerations lead us to the final conclusion that in the system of Maori education... we should provide fully a type of education that will lead the lad to be a good farmer and the girl to be a good farmer's wife.'

A consequence of this policy was that the curriculum in Maori schools emphasised agriculture and (to a lesser extent) manual and vocational training, and domestic training for girls. Few Maori pupils moved beyond primary level (about 8.4 percent in 1935), most of them defeated by the lack of specifically Maori-oriented secondary schools, the need to pay fees, the requirements of the proficiency exam, or parental discouragement.

The situation changed under Labour. Expenditure on education was increased after a period of retrenchment under the previous government. Rural schools were consolidated, their facilities improved and school transport organised. Secondary education was made free for every pupil, the proficiency exam was abolished, and the school leaving age was raised to fifteen.

It also became apparent that land alone would not provide livings for the entire Maori population, and that training for alternative occupations was urgently needed. The movement of Maori workers and later families into rural towns for essential war work underlined this fact. The Government's response was to build Native District High Schools that placed greater emphasis on vocational training such as wood- and metalwork. As a result of these efforts the number of Maori pupils at secondary schools increased, to 30 percent of those eligible by 1951. But the rate of training for skilled manual work remained low, and there was still a lack of emphasis on academic education and on preparation for the professions. Consequently few Maori entered white-collar occupations in the post-war years. Most remained farm workers, while a growing minority was joining the unskilled labour force in rural towns and in cities.

Another consequence of the segregation of Maori and Pakeha populations throughout the early years of the twentieth century was a continuing commitment on the part of Maori to Maori values and practices, and to specifically Maori religious observances, even though most Maori belonged at least nominally to a Christian church. Most denominations had separate Maori missions with Maori clergy and Maori congregations. Although it has been noted that formal church attendance tended to be lower than that for non-Maori, religion permeated Maori life far more intimately. Services were frequently held in the course of hui and tangi, committee meetings opened and closed with prayers, and the very status of training for the ministry or ordination tended to confer kaumatua rank in the Maori world.

The Church of England claimed the strongest Maori following throughout the first half of the twentieth century: 34 percent in 1926 and 32 percent in 1951 (the latter figure representing some 37,000 members out of a total of 115,600 declared religious adherents). The Ratana Church increased its membership spectacularly in the 1920s and 1930s to claim second place and a proportional peak of 20 percent in 1936. In the 1940s it dropped back to third place behind the Catholic Church, which held a steady 13 to 14 percent adherence. The other major affiliations in order of size were Methodist, Latter-day Saints and Ringatu.

Of the specifically Maori churches Ringatu was the strongest after Ratana with six percent in 1926, dropping to four percent in 1951. Numbers for the smaller denominations – Pai Marire, Wairua Tapu, and the followers of Te Whiti O Rongomai and Tohu Kakahi at Parihaka and elsewhere – fell away sharply to total less than 400 people by 1951. In one sense the statistics for the Maori churches are misleading, however: they do not show that many people belonged to a Christian denomination *and* a Maori church. In the Urewera, for example, many Tuhoe were Presbyterian and Ringatu; in Waikato Pai Marire practitioners were often also Methodist. Declared affiliation would usually depend on whether the circumstances were judged to be Maori or Pakeha; and the collection of census information was decidedly Pakeha.

Among the Maori sections of the Christian churches, denominational differences tended to be less defined and less important to members than among non-Maori sections. They were regarded far more as a reflection of the earlier spheres of influence decided upon by the churches' missionary arms (and, indeed, the major denominations retained the expression 'mission' to designate their Maori pastorates). Ecumenical services were a commonplace feature of tangi long before they achieved acceptance among Pakeha churchgoers.

Membership of a Christian denomination in no way precluded the observance of Maori values and religious practices. The Anglican, Methodist and Presbyterian Churches incorporated concepts such as tapu, noa and wairua into their liturgy because they had close Christian equivalents. With the exception for a time of Ratana and the Latter-day Saints, all churches allowed their rituals for the dead to be absorbed into the institution of the tangihanga; and tangi for the dead continued to be held throughout the twentieth century. Indeed for most Maori, tangihanga provided more regular opportunities for the observances of Maori ritual and marae ceremonial than any other occasion. All denominations devised prayers for circumstances in which traditional tohunga would have recited karakia: for sickness, death, misfortune, exorcism, setting out on a journey, blessing newly made objects. Water for blessing and ritual cleansing continued to be used in the manner it had been traditionally.

Adherence to Maori values persisted in other contexts to an extent that surprised Pakeha observers. Mana continued to be the quality that determined leadership status, though increasing weight was given to mana that was earned by achievement rather than that which was purely hereditary. The personal tapu of persons of rangatira rank continued to invite respect in Maori communities. People continued in Maori situations to place weight on personal identification through their genealogy. Muru, or sanctioned confiscations, took place in appropriate circumstances into the 1950s. And certain kinds of disputes between individuals and tribes were still settled by tatau pounamu, gifts of greenstone.

Discussion at hui continued to be held almost exclusively in Maori, to be structured according to the conventions of whaikorero, and to centre on the continuous preoccupation with whenuatanga, rangatira- tanga, whakapapa, mana and mana motuhake. Such discussions were surrounded and protected by marae ceremonial conducted according to the kawa of the tangata whenua. Whatever demographic and cosmetic changes the Maori people underwent in the first half of the twentieth century, they cloaked persistent commitment to traditional beliefs and practices, especially in the vicinity of turangawaewae or established marae.

Tribalism continued to be a dominating feature of Maori life, to the joy of those who *felt* tribal, and to the exasperation at times of those who felt Maori or who were Pakeha. Hence tribal rivalry led to disputes over authority and occasional slander in the Maori Battalion; Maori officials in the Department of Native Affairs had the greatest difficulty persuading people to adopt departmental policies if they (the officers) were from another tribal district; and well-meaning Pakeha who tried to get Maori information as distinct from tribal propaganda were often doomed to frustration. After spending half a lifetime compiling his *Dictionary of New Zealand Biography*, G.H. Schofield said in 1940: 'Maori history is sadly distorted and vitiated by the highly developed tribalism and the intense rivalries of the generations that the Maori have spent in New Zealand... the spirit of tribal pride moves even the broadminded Maori to ignore, if possible, and to gloss over if not, the vicissitudes of their own tribes and chiefs.'

What was a debilitating and destructive handicap from one point of view (in the above case a Pakeha one) could be a source of strength from another. Tribalism was the source of much of the group vitality and competitiveness of Maori life. And most Maori individuals continued to draw their identity and strength not from being Maori, but from being a known member of a particular hapu or tribe, and from being embraced by the people, history and traditions of that tribe. John Rangihau of Tuhoe, born into such a situation at Waikaremoana in 1919, expressed it in this way:

'These feelings... are my Tuhoetanga rather than my Maoritanga. Because my being Maori is utterly dependent on my history as a Tuhoe person... It seems to me there is no such thing as Maoritanga because Maoritanga is an all-inclusive term which embraces all Maori... I have a faint suspicion that [it] is a term coined by the Pakeha to bring all the tribes together. Because if you cannot divide and rule, then for tribal people all you can do is unite them and rule. Because then they lose everything by losing [the] tribal history and traditions that gave them their identity.'

CHAPTER SIX

TE AO HOU

THE NEW dAWN

Most tribes retain traditional recollections of one or even two migrations: that which brought their ancestors to New Zealand from the ancestral homeland Hawaiki; and that which took them from an earlier place of settlement to the one in which the hapu is now based, around its meeting houses and waahi tapu. From the time of World War II, however, most Maori families underwent a third migration, which took its members from small, largely rural Maori communities into the towns and cities of the nation, where the conventions of living were Pakeha-defined. It was a shift that brought compensations and trauma; eventual security and wider opportunities for some and cultural and emotional dislocation for others. It brought Maori and Pakeha into widespread contact for the first time since the wars of the 1860s, and with that contact came new demands, conflict, and a long apprenticeship of adjustment in which both peoples were forced for the first time to begin to know one another. By the 1990s that readjustment had led to a reassertion of mana Maori and a need to renegotiate the social contract between Crown and Maori, and Maori and Pakeha.

The relocation of the Maori population began in earnest during World War II when manpower regulations and the Maori War Effort Organisation opened up a diversity of labouring and manufacturing jobs not previously available generally to Maori men and women. In addition, the recreational options of city life created in some country areas what one observer called a 'fantasy contagion'. In 1936 only 11.2

percent of the Maori population had lived in urban areas. By 1945 this had risen to 19 percent, and by 1971 to 68.2 percent. In the 1980s the figure rose to over 90 percent and Maori had become an over-whelmingly urban people. The impact can perhaps be best visualised by consideration of the figures for individual cities. There were 1,766 Maori in Auckland in 1935, for example. By 1945 there were 4,903, and by 1951 7,621. In the same period the Wellington Maori population jumped from 341 to 1,570.

There was no single cause for the momentum which this migration built up. In periods of national prosperity the ready availability of well-paid but unskilled work was one attraction. It led to Maori taking manual jobs in large numbers in provincial towns and cities (in labouring, construction and freezing works, for example) – the kinds of jobs that would leave them vulnerable to unemployment in times of national economic downturn. Nor was it simply a case of the positive appeal of such work. There was also a negative factor in the economic decline of Maori rural communities brought about by the inability of Maori land alone to provide a living for a burgeoning population.

Ngata's land legislation had helped to sustain Maori communities in the 1930s and 1940s. It had come nowhere near 'solving' all the problems associated with Maori land, however. And with the population explosion that became apparent in the wake of World War II the deficiencies of that land as a source of employment and income became more obvious. Much of it was characterised by steepness, remoteness, high rainfall, unstable surfaces and other unfavourable features. Further, many of the dairy farms developed under Ngata's schemes proved to be uneconomic because of their size; many scheme workers found they could make considerably more money from casual labour on larger adjacent units, usually Pakeha-owned. These became steadily more profitable as a result of progressive mechanisation, which most Maori farmers could not afford.

In some areas land which had been on short-term lease to Euro-peans, with no provisions for compensation for improvements, was returned to Maori owners 'unscrupulously milked', in the words of one commentator. And, as if these difficulties were not enough, there were also those 'associated with ownership and control, grounded in a recent history of rapid and thorough cultural change, and related to a system of values which does not accord total priority to the Pakeha goals of efficiency and productivity.'

This is not to suggest that Maori farming as a whole was a failure. Far from it: some incorporations and individual farmers did spectacularly well. Nor was Pakeha farming by contrast an unqualified success. But the situation did create a cycle of circumstances that led to unforeseen problems in town and country: uneconomic Maori farming was an incentive for workers and families to move to towns and cities, and this process of depopulation made rural communities even less viable and urban migration by contrast still more appealing. And the combination of rural population displacement, urbanisation, and a relative lack of educational qualifications among Maori workers produced a brown proletariat in New Zealand cities, a situation that some commentators viewed as a dangerous ingredient in urban race relations.

J.G.A. Pocock, for example, wrote: '... we may be going to have ghettoes – the current term for urban areas where a distinctively pigmented minority have to live with bad houses, bad schools and unrewarding jobs – and, when faced with such ghettoes, the Pakeha may find that he is more prejudiced than he likes to believe... *whakama* may cease to be the mere feeling of shyness and inadequacy which it is now, and become instead a truly bitter sense of rejection; ideologies of alienation and ambivalence may arise, and the voice of some Maori (or Islander) James Baldwin may some day be heard.' This is an anticipation – by almost three decades – of Alan Duff's seminal novel *Once Were Warriors*.

Another major contribution to the urban migration was the monetary, recreational and lifestyle attractions of city life. These offered more choices, far more options for entertainment and hence – in the eyes of many – opportunities for a richer and fuller life. (In the eyes of a minority these same attractions were tantamount to confirming that cities were dens of temptation and iniquity.) Related to this was the feeling that opportunities for what was generally referred to as 'success' or 'betterment' lay in the city, not in the country.

There was also a follow-on process at work. A single member of a family might move to a city and experience immediate work and recreational advantages. They would report back to other members of the extended family, who would then join them over a period of time. These would in turn communicate with other members of the hapu or rural home community and set further migrations in motion. And so on. This was all part of the 'fantasy contagion'. It was not unlike older rural myths such as that about the streets of London being paved with gold. The reality rarely lived up to full expectations; but that did not stop either the fantasies or the migration.

The social and cultural consequences of this relocation were considerable. They brought a need for dramatic changes in the management of both Maori and wider national affairs. Urbanisation presented migrants newly arrived from rural areas with a set of Pakeha suburban mores not evident in Maori communities; there were difficulties associated with managing salaried incomes, budgeting, savings and investments; with accommodation, hire purchase and door-to-door salesmanship; there were instances of overt discrimination in employment, accommodation and hotel bars that arose from Maori and Pakeha becoming visible to one another and having to interact on a broad basis for the first time.

Urbanisation brought a need to redefine aspects of Maoriness: the nature of the extended family in the urban context; how to hold hui in the city; whether to take tupapaku 'home' to rural marae or to conduct tangihanga and burials in the city. There was also a need, for the first time outside war conditions, for people from differing tribal backgrounds to devise ways of cooperating with one another to solve specifically Maori problems. Differences of kawa had to be resolved, traditional suspicions and antagonisms discarded or submerged. Tangata whenua already swallowed up by urban expansion were at first unwilling to let people from other tribal backgrounds use existing marae facilities (Ngati Whatua in Auckland, for example, and Ngati Toa in Porirua). This fact and the absence of marae in new suburbs led to the conception and development of urban marae. In the process of addressing themselves to these problems Maori discovered that de-tribalisation could lead to multi-tribalism, and an intensification of a sense of Maoriness grew out of urban marae projects such as those at Maraeroa in Wellington and Hoani Waititi in West Auckland. For many Maori this experience was an unexpected joy and a source of additional strength and optimism.

Urbanisation brought to light aspects of Maori vulnerability in relation to non-Maori. In 1951, 57 percent of the Maori population was 20 years old and younger (as against 34.8 percent of the Pakeha population), which indicated a greater proportion of young dependants and non-wage-earners. In addition the Maori birth rate was considerably higher than that of non-Maori: 43.6 per 1,000 in 1955 as against 26. Most significantly, the vast majority of the Maori work force was in unskilled and lower income employment, especially agriculture and related industries (33 percent in 1951) and manufacturing (23 percent). Only 3.36 percent of Maori workers at that time earned £700 or more per year, compared with 18.6 percent of non-Maori. Conversely, in 1956 only 6.56 percent of the Maori work force held professional, managerial and clerical positions as against 26.69 percent of non-Maori.

All these factors combined to make Maori families more vulnerable as a group than Pakeha when wool prices fell a decade later and ended full employment. They created a circle of circumstances that was self-reinforcing and difficult to break: lower standards of educational attainment led to lower-income jobs or unemployment, which led to lower standards of housing and health, which led to higher rates of Maori crime, which led back to lower educational attainment and so on. Attempts to define these factors and their magnitude, and to devise new policies to deal with them, were not made until well into the 1960s.

In addition, all the conditions mentioned – especially poorer educational performance, lower incomes, poorer standards of housing and higher rates of crime – were ingredients for racial tension. They were seen by the wider community as 'Maori problems', and Maori were physically identifiable as a racial group. Pakeha were viewed by the media as individual New Zealanders; Maori as representatives of a race. And this, along with instances of overt discrimination against Maori in employment and accommodation, underlined why race relations had seemed relatively good in New Zealand from 1900 to the 1950s: not because of enlightened legislation or Pakeha altruism or even the Maori's capacity for adaption; but because the two races had been kept largely apart from one another.

Changing social and economic conditions in Maori life led to continued experimentation with different styles of leadership. The rangatira or hereditary basis for hapu leadership survived, but largely in rural areas. An increasing number of leaders such as Whina Cooper, whose basis for authority had originally been tribal and rural, made the transition to leadership in urban, multi-tribal Maori life.

Born Josephine Te Wake at Te Karaka on the Hokianga Harbour in 1895, she was the daughter of a leading Te Rarawa chief, Heremia Te Wake. From Heremia, Whina inherited mana, considerable ability, and an expectation that she would assume a leadership role among the Kai Tutae and Ngati Manawa hapu of Te Rarawa. After education at Whakarapa Native School and St Joseph's Maori Girls' College in Napier, Whina was in succession a teacher, a storekeeper and a farmer in the Hokianga district. She took her father's place after he died in the Influenza Epidemic of 1918, and by the late 1920s, based at Panguru, she was known as the most forceful Maori leader in the northern Hokianga.

When Ngata was seeking community support for his land development programmes Whina was an obvious ally, and she introduced and supervised the schemes in her area. She extended her expertise and her influence as a consequence of a second marriage in 1935 to William Cooper, a Ngati Kahungunu friend of Ngata who had represented the Maori people on the Royal Commission investigating Maori land in 1925.

After Cooper's death in 1949, Whina moved to Auckland to begin voluntary welfare work among Maori who had been moving steadily to the cities after World War II. She was elected first president of the Maori Women's Welfare League in 1951, a position she held for six years. After establishing local branches of the league throughout the country, and making a considerable impact in the education of Maori mothers in such matters as child-rearing and household budgeting, Whina Cooper turned the league into the only national Maori forum for discussion then in existence, and into the major non-political pressure group for representations to governments. (Both these roles were later assumed by the New Zealand Maori Council, established in 1962.) She was also especially active in securing adequate Maori housing in Auckland, in building urban marae, and in fundraising for voluntary welfare programmes, especially those organised by the Catholic Church.

In 1975 she established Te Roopu O Te Matakite and led the Maori Land March from Te Hapua in the far north to Parliament in Wellington, dramatising a national Maori determination not to lose any further land to Pakeha ownership. She remained a prominent Maori protest figure in the 1980s and 1990s, still adopting new causes and formulating representations to Ministers of Maori Affairs as she approached 100 years of age. She had departed from traditional patterns of Maori leadership in that her influence in the later years of her life sprang from her reputation as an urban and national Maori figure – as Te Whaea o te Motu or 'Mother of the Nation' – rather than from her localised or tribal position. She died in 1994 aged 98.

Another major training ground for non-tribal Maori leadership, in addition to preparation for church ministries, was the Public Service. There had been few Maori public servants prior to World War II, although those few exercised considerable influence: Raumoa Balneavis, a Ngati Porou, was for over twenty years secretary to successive Ministers of Native Affairs and became the most powerful force in his department; Pei Te Hurinui Jones of Ngati Maniapoto received his administrative training in the Native Land Court and later turned it to impressive use in land incorporation and development work; and Tipi Ropiha of Ngati Kahungunu, after a highly successful career in the Departments of Lands and Survey and Native Affairs, was appointed first Maori to head the Department of Maori Affairs in 1947. Later ministerial secretaries, especially Michael Rotohiko Jones of Ngati Maniapoto and John Grace of Ngati Tuwharetoa, were also major sources of influence behind the political scene.

After World War II, a large group of former Maori Battalion officers moved into Maori-related posts in the Public Service (men such as James Henare, Arapeta Awatere, Rangi Royal, Charles Bennett, Bill Herewini, Fred Baker, Moana Raureti and John Rangihau). Many of them completed university degrees with rehabilitation assistance after war service. Some, such as Henare Ngata and Harry Dansey, stayed outside the government and public service but dealt frequently with both in the course of tribal and incorporation administration. These men were an extension of the Young Maori Party model in the sense that they accepted the need for Western education and administrative skills so as to function within the bureaucracies of the government system. But, unlike their predecessors, they had seen the survival of Maori language, ritual and values into the second half of the twentieth century, and they were impatient with anything less than full equality with Pakeha citizens. One of their number, Rangi Logan, was to voice their feeling in the 1946 election campaign: 'We did more than our share at El Alamein and elsewhere... we shed our blood in two world wars.' If this had done nothing else, he declared, it had at least purchased the right to equality.

They accepted the *raison d'être* for the Department of Maori Affairs and the hierarchical structure by which it functioned, largely under Pakeha direction at district officer level. They accepted the basic concepts behind the land development schemes, incorporations, and the post-war welfare services. They also accepted that – to make a significant impact on the Pakeha-dominated systems of party politics and the Public Service – they had to lobby as Maori stating Maori take (causes); to be Waikato stating Waikato views or Ngapuhi representing Ngapuhi would have been to exercise relatively little influence over policy and legislation. In this they were assisted by their Maori Battalion background, which had helped them to view Maori as a people rather than as a group of competing tribal units, and by the process of detribalisation that accelerated after World War II as more and more families abandoned home marae and increasingly inter-married in cities with Maori from other regions.

These same Maori bureaucrats were to be challenged a generation later by a group of largely urban-based Maori dissidents, most of whom had backgrounds in tertiary education. They included Ranginui Walker and Pat Hohepa of the Auckland District Maori Council, Robert Mahuta of the Waikato kahui ariki, Koro Dewes and Sidney Mead of Victoria University, Tipene O'Regan of Ngai Tahu, and some leaders of Maori protest groups. These spoke out for Maori interests more emphatically and more abrasively than their predecessors, and they were to question whether the Public Service and local authority structures, with Pakeha reserving for themselves key policy-making positions, were the most appropriate ones to deal with the needs and aspirations of an indigenous Pacific people.

A major source of discontent among all Maori leaders in the wake of World War II was that successive governments were slow to perceive the changing conditions brought about by Maori urbanisation, and to respond to the representations of Maori pressure groups. Labour made some concessions by passing the Maori Social and Economic Advance-ment Act in 1945, which established tribal committees and the first Maori welfare officers. Labour also dropped the expression 'Native' from all official usage in 1947 and substituted 'Maori'.

When National came into power in 1949 they did so without any previous interest or conspicuous expertise in Maori affairs. They assisted with the setting up of the voluntary Maori Women's Welfare League in 1951, and in 1962 they passed the Maori Welfare Act which set up the New Zealand Maori Council (over the system of tribal committees established by Labour) and acted upon some of the recommendations of the Hunn Report of 1961. This latter had been commissioned but not actioned by the second Labour Government.

The Hunn Report was a milestone for its time. It was the first official act of recognition of the process of Maori urbanisation and it suggested policies to cope with the conditions that urbanisation presented. It assumed that the future of the two races and cultures was to blend, and that this was a desirable goal. Articulate Maori opinion attacked it on the grounds that Maori did not want to blend with Europeans and would not; and that Maori leaders had not been canvassed in the course of its preparation. The National Government accepted its recommendation that Maori houses should be 'pepper-potted' among general State housing, but this policy was later abandoned; Maori, even in cities, preferred to live in Maori surroundings, and many Pakeha turned out to be unenthusiastic about the prospect of Maori neighbours. The report's most successful consequences were the setting up of the Maori Education Foundation to help pupils through secondary and tertiary education, the extension of trade training facilities for Maori, and the provision for hostel accommodation and pre-employment courses for young Maori new to city life.

From the time of the publication of the Hunn Report, Maori leaders became increasingly aware that although Pakeha governments now spoke of integration as the ideal cultural blueprint for New Zealand, few Pakeha were actually prepared to tread the two-way street of integration by learning Maori language and customs. Assimilation and integration both required Maori to become Pakeha. The Maori had to learn everything about the English language and Western ways of living; there was no serious pressure on Pakeha to reciprocate. As a result Maori values and institutions had a lower status in New Zealand life than their Western equivalents.

Frequently when cases were made to Government or the Public Service for things such as the teaching of Maori language, a larger Maori content on radio and television, greater recognition of oral literature and provision for Maori methods for dealing with Maori offenders, these proposals were subject to what one Maori commentator called 'the Pakeha veto'. Maori were in many respects prevented from pursuing Maoriness because Pakeha-oriented institutions could see neither the value of nor the necessity for such measures; they were frequently dismissed as 'separatism', a potential source of social divisiveness. The agencies of the New Zealand system of government – in education, in law, in public works and in other branches of the Public Service bureaucracy – were committed to reflect Western values, criteria, practices and priorities rather than Polynesian ones. The more these factors were recognised and articulated in Maori quarters, the more they were resented. They led to the rise of urban protest groups: Maori organisations that articulated Maori considerations and needs, but which adopted Western rather than traditional modes of expression, such as demonstrations, picketing, petitions to Parliament and press releases.

The first such group to make its influence felt in the late 1960s was formed in Auckland, where Maori numbers were greatest and where the unpreparedness of government, local bodies and Pakeha individuals for Maori urbanisation was most apparent. Nga Tamatoa (the young warriors) grew out of the leadership of the Auckland University Maori Club, but its membership included young manual workers. Like the Maori Organisation on Human Rights established in Wellington slightly earlier, it was initially a reaction to the National Government's 1967 Maori Affairs Amendment Act, which gave the Maori Trustee additional powers to take control of Maori land, and which provided for land owned by fewer than four persons to pass into individual titles. The act was immediately attacked by Maori opinion as a high-handed (if well-intentioned) measure that lacked the support of the very people it purported to help.

Rapidly, however, both protest groups widened their campaigns to include the teaching of Maori language in schools, Maori control of Maori land and Maori finance, assistance for Maori offenders appearing unrepresented before the courts, an end to annual celebrations of the signing of the Treaty of Waitangi, and the severance of sporting links with South Africa. They were joined by Te Reo Maori, centred on Victoria University, which concerned itself primarily with the promotion of Maori language and literature and with the performance of the media, especially television, in dealing with Maori issues.

Te Roopu O Te Matakite (later Te Matakite O Aotearoa) grew out of the Maori Land March of 1975, which dramatised a determination not to relinquish further Maori land. Separate protest groups formed to campaign for the return of the Raglan golf course to Maori ownership (it had been seized by the Government and a community displaced for the building of a landing strip during World War II), and for the return of Bastion Point in Auckland to Ngati Whatua ownership. This last led to a 17-month occupation of the point in 1977–78, and the arrest of 200 protesters in May 1978 after the largest police operation in the country to that time. In 1979 the Labour Member for Northern Maori, Matiu Rata, resigned his seat and contested it as leader of the Mana Motuhake Movement, which presented a modest programme for Maori self-determination. He did not regain the seat but Mana Motuhake achieved second place behind Labour in all four Maori electorates in the 1981 General Election, the most spectacular launching of a political party since the appearance of the Ratana movement.

The cumulative effect of the activities of these groups was to focus media attention on Maori issues, to gradually radicalise such establishment organisations as the New Zealand Maori Council and Maori parliamentary representation, and to bring about major changes in the operations of the Departments of Education, Justice, Conservation and Maori Affairs. Additional Maori language courses were introduced in schools, kohanga reo or 'language nests' were set up for pre-schoolers, one-year teacher-training courses were established for native speakers of Maori, public funds became available for the renovation of marae, legal aid was offered for Maori offenders, a Race Relations Act was passed outlawing discrimination, and a Race Relations Conciliator's office was opened to deal with complaints about discrimination and to mitigate racial and cultural conflict.

Most importantly, the Waitangi Tribunal was established in 1975 to deliberate and rule on alleged breaches of the Treaty of Waitangi; in 1985 its powers were made retrospective to 1840. From this time it became the focus of Maori resource claims.

The National Government's major Maori policy measure was the establishment of the Tu Tangata (stand tall) programme in the late 1970s, a crash course to equip young Maori with additional vocational and living skills. By the early 1980s the Government had accepted the call for greater Maori determination of Maori issues and had assigned the redrafting of the unsuccessful Maori Affairs Act to Maori representatives and organisations. It made additional funding available for the promotion of Maori culture and literature. It had appointed a Maori to head the Department of Maori Affairs, Kara Puketapu, and a Maori Minister, Manuera Benjamin Couch of Ngai Tahu. It also appointed a Maori chairman of the Parliamentary Select Committee on Maori Affairs.

From the mid-1980s the Lange Labour Government took reform of Maori policy even further. The Department of Maori Affairs was split into a slimmed-down policy advice ministry, Manatu Maori, and the Iwi Transition Authority, created to transfer former departmental functions to Maori groups and other Crown agencies. This restructuring was completed when the Ministry of Maori Development, Te Puni Kokiri, was established in 1992 with former senior Army officer Wira Gardiner at its head.

Another aspect of State sector restructuring also had far-reaching consequences for Maori. The 1986 State Owned Enterprises Act had given the Waitangi Tribunal power to adjudicate on the status of land being transferred from government departments to SOEs. The following year, in a case arising out of this process, the Court of Appeal ruled that 'the principles of the treaty override everything else in the State Owned Enterprises Act, and these principles require the Pakeha and Maori treaty partners to act towards each other reasonably and with the utmost good faith.' This decision, and the references to the principles of the Treaty of Waitangi grafted on to amendments of such legislation as the Education and Conservation Acts, gave the treaty an explicit place in New Zealand jurisprudence for the first time.

In 1993 the Bolger-led National Government offered Maori the Sealords Deal, by which the Crown in effect purchased 20 percent of the nation's fishery for allocation to Maori tribes. The actual distribution was to be carried out by the Waitangi Fisheries Commission. In return, Maoridom was asked to drop its treaty-based claims to fisheries resources. This action was controversial enough. But the Government went further.

The following year it produced its so-called Fiscal Envelope proposals to settle all Maori resource claims by the year 2000 and to budget a total of one billion dollars of public funds for this purpose.

The scheme was rejected decisively by most Maori at a series of regional hui in 1995. Instead, most tribes opted to continue pursuit of claims through either the Waitangi Tribunal or direct negotiation with the Crown (and the Tainui tribes settled their raupatu or confiscation claim in this manner in 1995). They rebuffed both Government's suggested timetable for settlement and the notion that there should be a one billion dollar cap on such spending.

Because of the divisiveness of these proposals, Maori opposition to Crown actions and proposed actions built up a head of steam not seen since the more acrimonious Waitangi Day protests of the early 1990s. Protests in 1995 included the occupation of Moutoa Gardens in Wanganui and the burning of Takahue School in Northland. This level of protest did not persist, however. Compared with the conditions of earlier years, major and irreversible adjustments had been made within New Zealand society by the 1980s. Maori were a far more visible component of every aspect of the country's life, although still under-represented in the professions and in higher-income suburbs. Maori elements were increasingly apparent in the arts, literature and rituals of the nation. And, for the first time, its institutions were bending slowly but decisively towards Maori needs and aspirations. Nothing seemed more certain than that the momentum of these changes would increase.

·

MANA MAORI

THE RENAISSANCE

New Zealand in the early twenty-first century was a variegated and multicultural society. Those who identified with an Irish culture of origin sometimes differentiated themselves from those of predominantly English descent, for example; and those of Anglo-Celtic descent from those whose ancestors were Italian, Chinese or Samoan. Even Maori distinguished between those of their number who were tribal and those who were 'urban', and between those who were Tuhoe and those who were Ngapuhi or Ngai Tahu.

Despite this multi-ethnic texture, however, the country's citizenry still coalesced in two broad cultural streams: Pakeha in the case of those whose culture derived predominantly from Europe and the Judaeo-Christian heritage, and Maori for those descended from the original Iwi o te Motu who had come to New Zealand from the islands of East Polynesia. And as those from the former group prepared to enter the third millennium of time measured from the birth of Christ, tangata whenua could not but be conscious that their occupation of the Pacific dated from an even more ancient era and that their habitation of Aotearoa New Zealand was already entering a second millennium. And on this cusp of history New Zealand Maori were poised to take more pervasive and more authoritative control of their own lives than they had experienced since the nineteenth century.

That this shift in power was imminent near the start of a new Christian millennium was a consequence of the history and circumstances of the previous one hundred years. Apirana Ngata and his contemporaries in the Young Maori Party had eventually been content to see Maori living in rural communities separately from Pakeha, believing that this provided an opportunity for Maori culture, identity and confidence to recover after the trauma of nineteenth-century European colonisation of the country and its people. The land development schemes and cultural revival programmes of the 1920s and 1930s were interventions designed to protect and reassert Maori in traditional tribal rohe or territories.

The real Maori revival, however, that of the 1970s and 1980s, occurred as a result of urbanisation. Although the migration of rural Maori to towns and cities initially weakened the traditional bonds of whanau, hapu, iwi and language, it was a prerequisite for Maori once again to imprint their culture and values on the nation as a whole. Urbanisation eventually brought the possibility of Maori remaining Maori, and at the same time participating in mainstream New Zealand social, cultural and political life. Educational attainment at all levels began to improve slowly but steadily; the urban radicals of the 1970s set in motion the government-backed reforms that resulted in more widespread teaching of Maori language and culture; more Maori entered the Public Service, especially in education; Pakeha educators and writers, influenced increasingly by a growing number of Maori colleagues, began to stress the extent to which Maori experience had been ignored or misunderstood in the shaping of the nation's history and public policies; and from the mid-1980s the decisions of the Waitangi Tribunal and direct negotiations between disadvantaged iwi and the Crown began to compensate Maori for resources lost as a result of successive governments violating the principles of the Treaty of Waitangi or tolerating other activities that posterity would come to view as illegal or unethical.

No sooner had restored resources begun to reactivate iwi social and economic activity – and the Sealords Deal of 1993 and the Tainui Raupatu Settlement of 1995 were the first spectacular examples – than a near-revolution occurred in the national political arena.

Labour had retained its control of all four Maori parliamentary seats until Tau Henare (great-grandson of the first Maori MP of that name) won Northern Maori for the New Zealand First party in 1993. The election that followed, in 1996, delivered all of T.W. Ratana's 'Four

Quarters' and one new Maori seat to New Zealand First. For the first time in 64 years there were no Ratana-Labour members in Parliament. There were several reasons for this reversal in loyalties. Many Maori – especially rural or unskilled workers and beneficiaries – had been damaged by the monetarist reforms of the Lange Labour Government between 1984 and 1990. National, who continued and intensified these reforms for the period that Ruth Richardson was Minister of Finance in the early 1990s, did not present an appealing alternative for Maori voters. New Zealand First, on the other hand, was founded in 1992 and led by a Maori, former National cabinet minister Winston Peters. By 1996 large numbers of Maori voters were persuaded of Peters' commitment to addressing issues concerning Maori (especially under-achievement in areas such as employment and over-representation in disadvantageous health and crime statistics) and by the talent of largely younger New Zealand First Maori candidates.

The weight of their support, combined with that of a large bloc of elderly Pakeha voters disenchanted with Labour and with National's surcharge on superannuation, gave New Zealand First sufficient MPs to form a coalition government with National in 1996. In addition, the introduction of a Mixed Member Proportional representation system of government brought a further nine Maori list members into Parliament (four for Labour, two for the Alliance, one each for National and ACT, and still one more for New Zealand First). The new Parliament, there-fore, had fourteen Maori members, and three Maori (Peters, Henare and John Tuariki Delamere) in cabinet. Peters was also Deputy Prime Minister. The result was that Maori had an unprecedentedly strong voice in the nation's political executive.

At the same time Maori expectations of what their constituency might win back from the Crown, whose agencies were now committed to upholding the principles of the Treaty of Waitangi, rose sharply. In the 1990s the cry from a new generation of radicals, eventually taken up by the multi-tribal New Zealand Maori Congress, was for delivery of what the Treaty had called 'tino rangatiratanga'. The expression, an abstraction of the word for aristocrat, had been coined by the missionary Henry Williams and translated in the English version of the

Treaty as 'chieftainship'. By the 1990s, however, many Maori employed the term to describe the more corporate style of leadership that had evolved since the nineteenth century, in conjunction with the establishment of a Westminster-style Parliament in New Zealand, in which *all* Maori – not simply rangatira – had political rights. For some Maori, the modern meaning of tino rangatiratanga was sovereignty; to others it denoted a more nebulous expectation of Maori control of Maori lives and activities.

The National-New Zealand First Government failed, in the eyes of Maori constituents, to meet the high level of expectation that its unprecedented number of Maori MPs and cabinet ministers had raised. In addition, the coalition fell apart before the following election and four of the five Maori seat holders walked out of New Zealand First, thus abandoning the platform on which they had been elected. The revenge of voters was swift and deadly. In 1999 Maori votes moved en masse back to Labour, who had represented their constituency of interests for most of the previous sixty years. This swing assured the election of a Labour-Alliance coalition government. Maori expectations, however, remained high and would no longer be satisfied with rhetoric and platitudes. The pressure to deliver programmes sympathetic to Maori needs, and ones which close the gap between Maori and Pakeha achievement, was now on the Helen Clark/Jim Anderton-led administration.

As the twenty-first century began, it was apparent that the major issue engaging Maori and Maori, and Maori and Pakeha, in the years ahead would be reaching an accommodation about the meaning and implications of tino rangatiratanga, and about the exact nature of the partnership between Maori and the Crown promised in the Treaty of Waitangi and enshrined in legislation relating to such key sectors as education, health and conservation. For some New Zealanders it was a prospect fraught with apprehension; for others it promised ultimate social and cultural equity between Maori and Pakeha.

Tribal Location Map

Traditional tribal areas and locations resulting from nineteenth century tribal migrations (based on Appendices to the Journal of the House of Representatives, 1870).

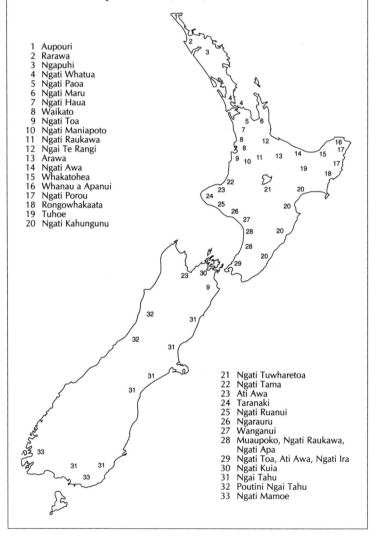

1 Aupouri
2 Rarawa
3 Ngapuhi
4 Ngati Whatua
5 Ngati Paoa
6 Ngati Maru
7 Ngati Haua
8 Waikato
9 Ngati Toa
10 Ngati Maniapoto
11 Ngati Raukawa
12 Ngai Te Rangi
13 Arawa
14 Ngati Awa
15 Whakatohea
16 Whanau a Apanui
17 Ngati Porou
18 Rongowhakaata
19 Tuhoe
20 Ngati Kahungunu

21 Ngati Tuwharetoa
22 Ngati Tama
23 Ati Awa
24 Taranaki
25 Ngati Ruanui
26 Ngarauru
27 Wanganui
28 Muaupoko, Ngati Raukawa, Ngati Apa
29 Ngati Toa, Ati Awa, Ngati Ira
30 Ngati Kuia
31 Ngai Tahu
32 Poutini Ngai Tahu
33 Ngati Mamoe

Sources and
Acknowledgements

An overview history is gleaned from more Maori informants, books, institutions and documents than I could list individually. I shall mention only those to whom I am most indebted.

For assistance over a period of time I wish to thank Sally Marshall-Tuwhangai, Sir James Henare, Robert Mahuta, Piri Poutapu, Te Uira Manihera, Heeni Wharemaru, Ngoi Pewhairangi, Whina Cooper, Joseph Cooper, Alex McKay, Marjorie Rau-Kupa, Bill Parker, Mairatea Tahiwi, Marie Smith and Sweet and Whenua Rehu; and, for special assistance with South Island Maori material, Irihapeti Ramsden and Sir Tipene O'Regan. E hoa ma, nau i waka aua te kakahu, he taniko taku.

Among colleagues whose work I have drawn especially from are Ann Parsonson, Janet Davidson, John Owens, M.P.K. Sorrenson, Keith Sinclair, Judith Binney, W.H. Oliver, Dick Scott, Ranginui Walker, Pat Hohepa, Ngahuia Te Awekotuku, Buddy Mikaere, Angela Ballara, Father E.R. Simmons and David Simmons.

The following are among the major publications I have consulted and in some instances quoted from:

For the book as a whole, I have drawn from *The Oxford History of New Zealand*, Geoffrey Rice (ed.), Oxford University Press, Auckland, 1990; and *The Maoris of New Zealand, Rautahi*, Joan Metge, Routledge and Kegan Paul, London, 1976.

Chapter One. *We, the Navigators: the ancient art of land-finding in the Pacific*, David Lewis, Australian National University Press, Canberra, 1972; *Ancient Voyagers in the Pacific*, Andrew Sharp, Paul, Auckland and Hamilton, 1967; *Maori Origins and Migrations*, M.P.K. Sorrenson, Auckland University Press/Oxford University Press,

Auckland 1979; *The First New Zealanders*, Phillip Houghton, Hodder and Stoughton, Auckland, 1980; *The Great New Zealand Myth*, D.R. Simmons, Reed, Wellington, 1976; *The Prehistory of New Zealand*, Janet Davidson, Longman Paul, Auckland, 1984; *Two Worlds*, Anne Salmond, Viking, Auckland, 1991.

Chapter Two. *The New Zealand Wars: a history of the Maori campaigns and the pioneering period*, James Cowan, two volumes, Government Printer, Wellington, 1922–23; *The Origins of the Maori Wars*, Keith Sinclair, New Zealand University Press, Wellington, 1957; *A Show of Justice: racial 'amalgamation' in nineteenth century New Zealand*, Alan Ward, Auckland University Press/Oxford University Press, Auckland, 1973; *The Shadow of the Land: a study of British policy and racial conflict in New Zealand, 1832–1852*, Ian Wards, Government Printer, Wellington, 1968; *New Zealanders at War*, Michael King, Heinemann, Auckland, 1981; *Cork of War: Ngati Toa and the British mission, a historical narrative*, Ray Grover, John McIndoe, Dunedin, 1982; *The New Zealand Wars and the Victorian Interpretation of Racial Conflict*, James Belich, Auckland University Press, 1986; *The Treaty of Waitangi*, Claudia Orange, Allen and Unwin/Port Nicholson Press, Wellington, 1987.

Chapter Three. *The Maori Population of New Zealand 1769-1971*, D. Ian Pool, Auckland University Press/Oxford University Press, Auckland, 1977; *Maori Houses and Food Stores*, William J. Phillipps, Dominion Museum, Wellington, 1952; *Traditional Maori Clothing: a study of technological and functional change*, S.M. Mead, Reed, Wellington, 1969.

Chapter Four. *Politics of the New Zealand Maori: protest and co-operation, 1891-1909*, John Williams, University of Washington Press, Seattle, 1969; *Ask That Mountain: the story of Parihaka*, Dick Scott, Heinemann/Southern Cross, Auckland, 1975; *Education and Identity: a study of the New Zealand Maori Graduate*, Thomas K. Fitzgerald, New Zealand Council for Educational Research, Wellington, 1977; *Mihaia: the prophet Rua Kenana and his community at Maungapohatu*, Judith Binney et alia, Oxford University Press, Wellington, 1979; *The Autobiography of a Maori*, Reweti Kohere, Reed, Wellington, 1951; *Man* of Two Worlds: Sir Maui Pomare, J.F. Cody, Reed, Wellington, 1953; Te Rangi Hiroa: the life of Sir Peter Buck, J.B. Condliffe, Whitcombe and Tombs, Christchurch, 1971; Ratana: the Man, the Church, the Political Movement, J. McLeod Henderson, Reed/Polynesian Society, Wellington, 1972; Te Puea, Michael King, Hodder and Stoughton, Auckland, 1977; Kotahitanga, the Search for Maori Political Unity, Lindsay Cox, Oxford University Press, Auckland, 1993.

Chapter Five. Maori Schools in a Changing Society: a historical review, J.M. Barrington and T.H. Beaglehole, New Zealand Council for Educational Research, Wellington, 1974; Challenge for Health: a history of public health in New Zealand, F.S. Maclean, Government Printer, Wellington, 1964; Challenge and Response: a study of the development of the Gisborne East Coast region, W.H. Oliver and Jane M. Thomson, East Coast Development Research Association, Gisborne, 1971; Integration or Identity? Cultural interaction in New Zealand since 1911, M.P.K. Sorrenson, Heinemann, Auckland, 1977; Amiria: the life story of a Maori Woman, Amiria Stirling and Anne Salmond, Reed, Wellington, 1976; Te Ao Hurihuri, Michael King (ed.), Hicks Smith/Methuen, Wellington, 1977.

Chapter Six. A New Maori Migration: rural and urban relations in northern New Zealand, Joan Metge, Melbourne University Press, Melbourne, 1964; The Maori and New Zealand Politics, J.G.A. Peacock (ed.), Paul, Auckland and Hamilton, 1965; The Maori in the New Zealand Economy, G.V. Butterworth, Department of Industries and Commerce, Wellington, 1967; Tihe Mauri Ora, Michael King (ed.), Methuen, Wellington, 1978; Race Against Time, Hiwi Tauroa, Human Rights Commission, Wellington, 1982; Ka Whawhai Tonu Matou, Ranginui Walker, Penguin, Auckland, 1990.

Index